Zita Fontaine is a sociologist, writer and an abuse survivor. She rewrote her own narrative of narcissistic abuse and launched a career in writing to heal and help other survivors. She writes no-fluff, no-nonsense pieces about abuse, feminism and relationships on medium.com with thousands of loyal readers.

ZITA FONTAINE

A BOX
FULL OF
DARKNESS

THE NO-NONSENSE GUIDE TO UNDERSTAND
AND MOVE ON FROM NARCISSISTIC ABUSE

ISBN: 9798644489442
Imprint: Independently published

Cover design by: Fabrikate

To Om, who gave me hope.

Someone I loved once gave me
a box full of darkness.
It took me years to understand
that this too, was a gift.

—MARY OLIVER

Table of Contents

1. OPENING THE BOX FULL OF DARKNESS

Abuse Is In The Moments Leading Up To Violence

The best and most terrifying instances of life are when you stop being yourself while still conscious. Those sweet moments of ecstasy when your body and mind lose contact, and for a fleeting second that feels like a lifetime, your conscious and subconscious self becomes one.

Disconnecting from reality, checking out from consciousness with a lingering feeling of being halfway here and halfway nowhere: the wide-eyed clarity of the nanosecond before the orgasm of your life. The minute that blurs into eternity, right before your blackout on that Friday night after the 15th shot. The punch of adrenaline hitting you in the chest that you feel as you jump from an airplane with a parachute, the ground closing in on you inevitably, but the freedom is worth the fall, and even the crash.

This is how I imagine death—the moment before you slip away, a final moment of clarity before the unknown, not knowing everything that is too short to remember and too final to tell anyone about. A promise of bliss in the face of all horrors, that might or might not devour you.

This is also how I imagine drowning—weighed down by the things you love, the things that bring life. A final struggle of limbs and lungs and veins and vertebras—the struggle to decide whether to give up and fight or let go and leave.

And this is how I experienced love. Love that lifted me to such great heights that I lost sight of the patchwork of reality below. Love that dragged me through the mud, leaving me spent and torn by the pavement, inhaling ditch water, and exhaling agony.

This is the love we had. That fleeting ecstatic frenzy, this mind-blowing, earth-shattering love, filled with sparks, fireworks, rainbows and butterflies—a sweet second of heaven just before the lethal storm hit with full force; the final clarity of reality, hurt, pain, and terror.

• • •

"I know it's too soon, but I fell in love with you." The words lifted me up and dragged me down all at once. How is it even possible to make space for such a vast ocean of conflicting feelings, crashing in on each other, rendering me speechless, helpless, and afraid? My brain froze, then my thoughts were rushing; locked in a tiny space, bouncing off my reason, taking another angle to rain over me. It took forever to lift my eyes to meet his—I blushed, trembled, and finally smiled.

I wanted this; wanted him to fall in love with me. I felt like I was heading there, but mine was like a freight train, slow and unstoppable; the weight of the emotions overwhelming and incredibly burdensome. *It was too soon.* Too soon for me to feel, and too soon for him to say. It mirrored the unreality of my own feelings and questioned everything rational. Am I allowed to be in a love story like this? Can it really happen that we just met a few weeks ago and he became such an integral part of me that life seemed impossible without him? Reason fighting emotion. Fuck reason.

· · ·

"You know, we already have a baby… somewhere in space and time. He's just not born yet at this moment, but time is relative and no matter how much we need to bend it, we will get there. There are things in life that you cannot escape from. I don't know how I know it; I just know."

5

"Don't put that lipstick on." I froze mid-movement, unable to hide the frustration and fear that clouded my eyes for less than a second. I looked into his eyes in the mirror, raised my brows with an unspoken question, demanding an explanation without a word. *"How will I kiss you then?"* He smiled a mischievous half-smile and leaned in to kiss and gently bite my neck.

It was more than him wanting to kiss me, and as much as I wanted to buy his reasoning, I knew he was having a bad day. We called his pre-aggressive moments—when, as he explained, his demons came out to play—"moody". I put away the lipstick, toned down my eyeshadow, and decided not to wear perfume. I changed into a simpler dress, with no cleavage, and put my heels back into the wardrobe, slipping my feet into plain black ballerinas. I slouched, too. I wanted to be even smaller, shorter, less of an attraction.

We shouldn't have gone out that day. Meeting my colleagues and friends was an idea that initially thrilled him. Until it started to make him feel small and inferior. Until he started throwing accusations around. Until somehow, I, the love of his life, the mother of his child, became an object of his disgust.

"Did you fuck any of them?"

"What?" My heart started beating faster.

"I am asking you a simple question, the least you can do is tell me the truth. Did you fuck any of your colleagues? Am I going to become drinking buddies with anyone who fucked you?"

"Let's just go home, please. You're moody, I don't want you to make a scene, these are my colleagues."

We got out of the taxi, a one-minute walk from where we were supposed to meet my colleagues. I wanted to turn around and go home, hide under a rock, run away. He smiled smugly, grabbed my hand a little too hard, and dragged me to meet my friends. I forced a smile.

"I need a drink. Get me a double vodka."

"But... we agreed that you wouldn't drink when you are moody, at least not shots... love... it makes it worse. I don't feel comfortable."

I was pleading with him.

"Okay, which one did you fuck?" He was looking around, raising his voice, sizing up the guys. *"That one with the beard? He looks dirty enough to want to fuck you senseless."*

"I'm getting you your drink, just stop this nonsense right now."

"Good girl." He spat the words. He hated me so much it made me sick.

• • •

We ran out of bread, milk and butter, and yes, baby formula. I was making a list in my head—we

7

must go out grocery shopping. I had a million things on my mind. My new job was boring but gave me a lot to do. It was part-time but lasted more than four hours each day. We needed the money. I was the only breadwinner while he had been unsuccessfully looking for a job for the past four months.

When I arrived at the flat, carrying our six-month-old daughter, he didn't even get up to greet me. I poked my head in the room, it was filled with smoke. He was lying on the bed, watching something on his laptop.

"Umm, hi, baby. What's going on?"

"I took a couple of Rivotrils." He slurred the sentences and smiled in slow motion. He was in his bathrobe, a cigarette in his hand. We never smoked inside.

The baby stirred in the baby seat. When I put her in her crib, she smiled in her sleep and for the shortest second the world looked beautiful in the reflection of her tiny, angelic face. It was 3 p.m. I had less than an hour to pick up the girls, grocery shop, cook and clean, and check a presentation for work. I let out a don't-fuck-with-me sigh; I couldn't deal with his Rivotril trip right then.

"I am f-f-fine, come on now, give me a kiss." He looked sheepish.

"How many did you take?" I asked, frantically checking the blister pack, not realising I needed to keep tabs on the number of remaining tablets. All I knew was that he should take two a day; this was the strongest version available.

"N-not sure." He laid back on the bed. I took the cigarette out of his hands before the pillow caught fire. I helped him under the covers and started to shake. I couldn't believe he was doing this to me. *"Maybe eight, or… 10? And I took some sleeping pills too."*

"I'm calling an ambulance." I was fumbling for my phone, unable to see from rage mixed with fear.

He sobered up for a minute, coming out of his drug haze. *"Don't you do that, bitch. I'll kill you."*

I was looking for the sleeping pills, but I couldn't find them anywhere. We didn't even have sleeping pills at home. He just said it to worry me.

Then he eased back into the galaxy of benzodiazepines, lost in the hope of finding himself. He drifted away, mouth open, leaving behind the world where everything was cruel and against him. He left for a place that loves him and accepts him, a universe that doesn't hurt but takes him in a huge, rubbery grey embrace. Time stopped, and space as we know it ceased to exist. The dimensions seemed ridiculous. Life seemed ridiculous. I seemed ridiculous.

He looked so peaceful, and as I looked at his face, the love I had stopped feeling for him bubbled up inside me. I had been pulling the weight for both of us, dying under the pressure of time and space and tasks and emotions. It felt like an ocean swallowing me, pulling me under, the pressure increasing with every second as I sank deeper, crushing my chest, contracting my heart, and making my veins explode.

How can you not drown when you are inhaling water? How can you not sink when the love you once felt, and can't let go, becomes a block of concrete, shackled to your feet?

The baby moaned in the other room, pulling me out from underwater. Survival is overrated; responsibility trumps everything.

I grabbed the baby, ran out of the flat, did the grocery shopping, picked up my daughters from school... so many things to do. I called his psychiatrist, who didn't answer. I called my cousin, whose wife is a doctor, and he didn't answer. I contemplated who else to call. What if I'd already wasted too much time? What if he... what if he dies? What if he lives?

When his psychiatrist called me back, she said he was in no imminent danger; didn't need to have his stomach pumped. He would sleep for a couple of days. She ended the conversation with, *"Don't mind him, he will be fine. Please, take care of yourself. You need it more."*

. . .

He had a thing about having everything in precise order, a kind of OCD that only worked against me. The spoon on the kitchen counter needed to be parallel to the line of the sink. If there was more than one dirty spoon, they both had to be aligned. He also hated the sponge in the sink, the kettle boiling the same water again. He hated if I left the door open when he wanted it to be closed or splashed a tad more milk into his coffee than he wanted. What had been perfect yesterday didn't cut it today, so I only made good coffee once in my life. Every other time it was too hot, too cold, too sweet, too bitter, or the mug was just not right—and it ended up on the floor, forcing me to clean up coffee splatters from the wall with bleeding fingers. How can a small amount of coffee make such a mess?

He had a thing about things needing to be parallel. As if having things in order on the outside could have fixed the turmoil of his nasty thoughts and even nastier actions. As if the parallelism of two spoons could have mended the disastrous disorder that was firing up his brain cells, ruining the healthy connectedness of the synapses, stopping him from being the inherently good person he believed he was.

I had a thing about knives: They freaked me out. It started when we had a heated argument in the kitchen, and he told me in a hushed voice that he really felt like hitting me. I saw his fist balled up, and a crazy spark in his eyes. He also added, in a forcibly calm voice, that he could never kill anyone; hitting and kicking yes, but not killing. Then he glanced sideways at the bread knife on the counter. My mind froze—I was never afraid of him hurting me physically, and even thought that him confessing he wanted to hit me but holding himself back, was a good sign.

But the side-glance at the knife? That sent shivers down my spine. It started my obsessiveness about order, and parallels, and knives always being in the drawer, and sponges always out of the sink. I got sick if I realized I had left a ball of hair in the bathroom; started to shiver when I saw that the shower gel was running out, forcing me to make late-night trips to buy toiletries, and doing midnight cleaning sprees. *I also needed to make sure that all the knives were put away.*

. . .

It was hope—the most powerful drug in the whole universe, and my narcotic of choice. It made me irrational and able to fall in love with him every day. If it was a good day, our eyes locked with the promise of eternity and bliss. If it was a bad day—and after a while, there were only different levels of bad—I simply hoped I would find him again, lure him back from his demons, hold his hands, and it would be enough.

I refused to believe that nothing was enough; that no effort I made could cure our tragic, futile love triangle: me loving him and him loving himself.

And under this unrequited self-love of his narcissistic, sick mind, there was a sticky film of hatred that clung to everything he touched: memories, feelings, relationships, connections, hopes, and love. All of it tainted and dirtied while he eternally searched for validation, willing to ruin everything for the promise of a new fling, the admiration of a fresh pair of eyes.

My love was never enough. I was never enough. Us as a family was never enough. The work I put into our relationship was never enough. It took me too long to realize that, despite my best intentions, I was only digging us deeper into the black hole we had fallen into together, when we thought we were falling in love.

We were living on the edge, standing on the precipice, clinging to that sweet second of heaven just before the lethal storm hit us full force.

. . .

"I am not going to get you in trouble." My voice is shaking. *"Please let us go."*

"Come to bed, I am not going to hurt you anymore. I love you; I didn't want to hurt you. I am so sorry." He is sobbing.

I am sitting on the edge of the bed, with my back to him. I am not running anymore. He is calm now; I don't have to be afraid. I know he won't hurt me. The adrenaline of fear that kept me on my feet is slowly leaving my body, and I feel eternal fatigue creeping in. My soul is yawning, my body is yearning for senseless sleep.

"Just lie down here, I know I scared you. I don't know what happened."

He pulls me onto the bed. He's caressing my face and my tummy. I know he will undress me in no time. I want to think that I don't want him to touch me, after what he just did to me. But I can't talk and don't feel anything, can't even want or not want. Today I have done more than enough for a lifetime. I survived. We survived. I tried to run but he didn't let me. I could run, but I can't. Not today. Maybe tomorrow. I can check my bruises tomorrow and decide whether I will go to the police. Tomorrow I will figure it all out. I just can't do it today.

For today, I am safe. I am not afraid anymore. I no longer fear the future because the past has already brought everything I feared. I am still me but am seconds from losing myself—giving myself to something bigger that will eat me whole, devour me, and burn me alive. I am hurting, my muscles are aching, more exhausted than a body should be able to stand. I suck in some air and relax, still alive. Drowning, but alive for the moment.

I tried to make this relationship work for both of us. I gave sweat, tears, and broken bones for it. I gave my all until there was nothing left to give. Now I have to run, and I will… tomorrow. Just before I drift away, into an oblivious sleep, it crosses my mind that I put the knives away.

People always think abuse is violence. But abuse is in the moments leading up to it.

It's not the facts that drive you crazy, it's the lingering emotions that precede, surround, and follow the fragments of reality. It's not the knife that ever hurt me—it's the possibility of bleeding out on a rug, stabbed to death by someone who was supposedly the love of my life. It's not the bruises that were hard to heal—it's the string of nightmares, reliving all the blows that took away my sense of safety, even after I was secure, alone, and far away from harm. It's not that it's over that kills me, it's that I lost years of my life, my dignity, my self-esteem, my hijacked agency. It's not even the violence that is the most terrible aspect. It's the slurred words, imperceptible glances, and microscopic gestures that add up, drop-by-drop, to fuel an unstoppable missile bound to destroy me.

I did survive, but not for survival per se. I survived because responsibility trumps despair anytime.

A Box Full of Darkness

Someone I loved once gave me
a box full of darkness.
It took me years to understand
that this too, was a gift.

—*MARY OLIVER*

I am not one you could ever see being abused—or at least I thought I wasn't. I am strong and smart, I have two university degrees, I speak 4 languages, I am educated, I have always been able to make my own living ever since I moved out from home at the age of 22. I've always had a job, a huge circle of friends, a supportive family. I have always had everything that was bound to protect me from falling victim to abuse. And then again, for there are no rules for abuse, I was wrong. *There is no such thing as an average abuse victim.*

I used to be arrogant about it. Of course, not in an open way. I have always been much more polite and empathetic towards people than that, but deep down inside I thought: if he hurts you, girl, you need to move on, move out, have some dignity and do something about it. And I believed it, too. That all it takes is just one single decision to end a nightmare and resurrect yourself from it, I thought. I was so wrong.

This is my story. It is to tell you about how abuse happens gradually and how it is never the fault of the victim, no matter how easy it can be to blame them. It is about how my perspective was shifting, how long it took me to realize it, to accept that it's wrong, to muster up the courage to leave, to refrain myself from going back.

Abuse does not start by being abused. To the contrary. When I met my ex, he was everything I have ever wanted in a man, in a relationship. I believed that there had to be someone out there for me who would treat me right, who would know the right answers even before the question was asked, who would care about me, who would love me, and with whom I could learn to love myself. And there he was. He wasn't even my type, but we connected at the first moment. He was charming and funny, interesting and interested. He listened to what I said, he wanted to get to know me and looked at me like he just won the lottery. I fell for him. I thought I won the lottery too. It was too good to be true.

When something is too good to be true, it usually isn't. Lesson learned.

I can't remember when the beginning of the end was exactly. Was it when he first ridiculed me, when he first pushed me, when he beat me up, when he broke my rib when kicking me through the room, when he touched my daughter inappropriately or when he left for months and then came back smiling—like nothing had happened? I don't know. I don't even know when I lost him. Somewhere along the way I didn't only lose him, or a father to my baby, *but I totally lost my own way.* And at that point, I did not see a way back to life. I didn't want to live. I was broken, wrecked, damaged. I was afraid and I had no strength at all, no hope, no faith, nothing.

I wasn't myself—he took that from me. Day after day. Word after word. Slowly peeling away everything I used to believe in—the goodness in people, the hope, the trust, myself. Brainwashing doesn't happen overnight. But if you hear something enough times it becomes part of your personality and starts to define you.

It was hell. And I was still there. I didn't want to leave, and I didn't want to stay. I wanted him to change back to that charming man I fell for, who reappeared after an abusive event for some hours, showing me the same love and care I wanted so much. I wanted to believe him when he said he would change. And I couldn't leave because he told me I was fat and ugly and disgusting, that my personality was horrible, I was a monster, and this was why I didn't have friends. I was an awful daughter, and this was why my mom was not around. According to him, I was stupid, this was why I would lose my job and the custody of my daughter.

But then some more abuse came, more hurt, more threats, words and knives and life or death situations. I needed to run from him and that was the best thing that could happen. I needed to pull myself together, for pure survival, in fight or flight mode. I quit my job, I changed flats, I changed my phone number and email address. And I ran. It was painful but after several times of letting him back in my life, I finally chose me. I denied any promise he tried to give, and I said yes to my own life, to my future. I was terrified and broken, but there was no way I was going back to the hell he put me through.

The only way was to move forward. Healing takes a lot of time after a breakup, it always does. But especially after one with a dangerously distorted individual with a severe personality disorder, where you were chewed and spit out a thousand times, where your self-esteem is demolished, where hope and faith are as unattainable as a bright future. For me, it took years and I am still healing from it. From the PTSD, from the flashbacks, and sometimes from missing him—even though the man I miss may have never existed.

I forgave him, but I will never forget what he put me through. I forgave him because I could not afford to live a life that was defined by hatred, anger and rage. He gave me more strength and grit than anyone in this life; the hell he unleashed on me and within me shaped me more than any self-help, self-reflection ever could have.

I am still in hiding. I am very protective about my social media presence; I write under a pen name; I do not comment anywhere publicly; *I am not to be found.*

But I am here. I am alive. I am doing better than ever. I am not broken anymore. I was broken, and now I patched myself back together, the Kintsugi way.

Kintsugi is the Japanese art of repairing broken pottery with lacquer dusted or mixed with powdered gold, silver, or platinum. As a philosophy, it treats breakage and repair as part of the history of an object, rather than something to disguise.

I survived it, but I refuse to call myself a survivor. I refuse to let him define me this way, not anymore. And I don't blame myself anymore for not seeing the red flags. I am here, prouder and stronger than ever and I am not looking back.

I am passing on everything I have learnt; I owe me and you this. I went through hell and back and although it doesn't make sense why I had to, I cherish the empowerment that came from it. I am happy that I am stronger than ever. I am not the woman I used to be—and I am grateful for the pain that made me grow.

This is my box full of darkness. I never asked for it. It taught me more about life, relationships and myself than anything ever could have in my life. I didn't want this darkness—*but it was a gift.*

Reality Kicking In

I wanted to understand what happened. I wanted to see where it all went wrong. I wanted to take it all back, go back to square one. I wanted to feel again. I wanted to know if it was real. If he was real, if my love was real, if our love was real.

I delved into the abyss of everything I could find online—starting from 'how do I get an ex back', 'how do I get revenge', 'to why do I always fall for bad boys.'

The first weeks went by in a blur—I read dozens of articles and books about relationships, heartbreak, love and loss. It didn't make any sense. I felt I was going crazy. I missed him and I was dying from the pain.

I came across an article that explained the biochemical nature of falling in love and how love can be addictive. It talked about how love hijacks the brain and causes withdrawal symptoms in case of an abrupt breakup.

It was written so eloquently and clearly explaining my pain that I started to read more from the author (Shahida Arabi), who went through narcissistic abuse. Her words resonated with me too much. I was devouring the words she had written, article after article. And as the words reached my brain I started to scream inside—this unknown woman was writing about *my* life. She knew what I was going through. She painted the picture of *our* awful Christmases and she knew all of *his* words. She knew it all.

I thought I was alone in this—and suddenly a whole universe opened up in front of me—with predictable patterns, sentences and behaviours. A whole universe of hurt and pain and frustration.

I joined a support group I found on Facebook and to my utter horror, it became soon apparent that there are more like me—women with the same bruises on their bodies and in their souls. Women in decade-long suffering. Women of all ages and statuses. Women from every corner of the world. And then men too. All of them confused, hurt and broken.

Some were ahead of me in their healing journey, *giving me the hope that it would get better.*

That community became my lifeline. Reading others' stories let me know that I am not alone, that I am not crazy, that I am not the one to blame here. I soon made friends and I found a safe space to vent and cry. It was an amazing group of temporarily broken powerful women—and I was one of them, finally belonging somewhere after years of feeling isolated and alone.

I continued to buy books and I read more articles. I subscribed to newsletters. I read everything I could. I followed their advice—I tried everything to speed up healing. Little did I know that with him leaving me, it wasn't yet over—and there were more months and years to endure.

Awareness, Distance and Healing

We rarely see abuse coming. Its nature prevents us from seeing clearly or acting on it when we are already lucid to recognise reality. It's like a lightning bolt striking you out of the blue, leaving you speechless, desperately looking for answers and explanations, only to find even more confusion.

How could you grasp that someone who should love you and protect you is out to get you and ruin you—for one reason or the other? How could you understand that the one you care about is the one who will hurt you most? *Love says: I could hurt you, but I won't.* Love is about letting someone so close that we expose our most vulnerable parts in the hope that they won't cause us damage. *Abuse lies: I won't hurt you.* But eventually they do. Because abuse is about power and control.

I went through every typical step of narcissistic abuse.

And then I spent years trying to fix myself. I did everything I could to get back to myself, to grow from it, to survive and thrive. Our healing journeys are all different. The timing is different. The phases are different. We choose our journey, but we can't dictate the pace—it happens when it happens.

Healing is an upward spiral. Like grief. It's not linear. It can go in circles for weeks or even months until you take the first step forward. You can get thrown back to square one in a split second, or so it feels that way. There is no deadline for healing. It's your journey and yours alone. Take your time and use whatever you have to make it happen—and at some point, it will get better. Take it step-by-step, do it at your own pace.

I started to turn to art, music and sports. Finally, I turned to writing—the thing I have always done and always wanted to do, yet I never thought I would ever become a writer. *Words are powerful.* They have the power to hurt and the power to heal. I am using the power of words to heal myself and to provide others with the information that they might need to get better, to get back to life that is worth living.

I am not a healthcare professional—I am a writer, who is also an economist, with a degree in Sociology. This book and the suggestions in it are based on my learnings, my personal experiences together with research material and advice from fellow abuse-survivors.

The three most important things that I will cover here are awareness, distance and healing.

It starts with awareness

There were lucid moments when I knew perfectly clearly that I was being abused. I knew that this was not the life I wanted; he was no longer the man I wanted around me. It wasn't even life. The tricky part was to realize that it was the addictive nature of the abuse cycle and the intermittent reinforcement that made me addicted and attached to him, and it wasn't him or the relationship. It was a bitter pill to swallow. No matter how much I wanted this relationship, how much I wanted him, and how much I wanted it to work, I had to see and understand how he was manipulating me and made me believe that what we had was special. It didn't matter how every cell in my brain soaked in cocaine-like chemicals pushed me towards him, I needed to open my eyes and face reality.

It wasn't easy—it never is, with any addiction. And we should never underestimate the brain on drugs—even if it's "natural" drugs. But just realising that it is an addiction was already a huge step forward.

Through the following pages, to help you become more aware and educated, I will deep-dive into narcissism and its manifestation. I will show you how to recognise narcissism, what the signs are and why it is so difficult to notice when you are being abused.

I will show you the dynamics of an abusive relationship with a narcissist—how they behave, why they do what they do, what are the common patterns that unmistakably point to a broken relationship with a narcissistic individual.

I will show you what life looks like with them and why it is difficult to endure it.

Distance and zero contact

Coming off of the addiction was hard. It was similar to stopping a drug cold turkey. My brain was screaming for it, and it grabbed every opportunity to get what it wanted, to get back to it, no matter how much it would hurt after. Just like with any other addictive substance. It was a slow process, and I was dying inside. Everything I ever wanted was taken away.

But there was just simply no other way. It took weeks for the biochemical loop to break, for the hormone levels to get back to their normal 'non-cocaine-haze' state. And as the chemical induced fog was lifting, I started to see things for what they were. I started to get back in touch with reality, shaking my head in disbelief, as if I was waking up from a bad dream.

Distance was needed to break the addiction and get back to myself. The most important part of it was zero contact. Zero—as in zero. Any attempt and any heartfelt sentence, text message, any romantic gesture would have sent me back spiralling downward. I know, because it wasn't the first time I tried.

No contact also meant a mental cut-off from the thoughts. It is not enough to block someone on social media, remove ourselves from the physical proximity—a much harder bridge-burning is necessary too. To stop thinking about them, stop wondering what they might be doing, who they might be with. It means keeping so busy that you don't have the time or energy to think about them. It means exhausting yourself with every possible thing, just to be able to sleep at night without missing them to death.

I will talk about the importance of distance and no contact, to break the seemingly unbreakable bond—to gain enough clarity to move on. I will explain how no contact is in the little things and how it is imperative to stay away to be able to heal.

Healing comes only after

The worst part was still to come. After I started to see clearly and I showed every symptom of being abused (PTSD, depression, anxiety, flashbacks, etc.), I also began to feel things I hadn't allowed myself to feel such as shame, fear, humiliation, loss of contact with myself. *I didn't know who I was.* I didn't know anymore if I was still myself from before or someone who changed into a monster. Months went by; coping mechanisms were tried and tested, some failed, some stayed. It took me a long time to separate myself from him, when I could tell myself that I am no longer his to destroy.

No matter how long the healing takes, no matter how it feels to be thrown back to square one over and over again, you need to take your time. You need to learn to trust again—despite everything that you experienced. You need to learn to love again. *You need to learn to love yourself again.* You need to learn to find ways to express yourself again.

I will talk about the healing process, the power of your mind to get you through the worst of it. Healing is inevitable—you can, and you will heal. You can't speed up the process, but you can use this time to reconnect with yourself, to find new strength and agency within you.

2.WHY IS IT SO HARD TO RECOGNIZE ABUSE?

Is Everyone Around Toxic?

One of life's greatest challenges is to be around people who are draining your energy, who are non-supportive and who are just plain difficult. As if life wasn't complicated enough—to make ends meet, to find your purpose, to find joy—there are certain types of individuals who make it difficult to live your life with. No matter if we are talking about family, friends, colleagues or your partner—you deserve to have people in your life who you enjoy spending time with, who help you and support you and who don't deplete you.

But with a tendency for people-pleasing behaviour and the fact that we are taught that self-care is a bad thing, we might fail to notice toxic people until it's too late.

The biggest problem with toxic individuals is that it's close to impossible to see the signs of their distorted character immediately. Looking back on it, we usually notice their toxicity only when it's too late. The signs become obvious in hindsight, and it's plain to see how those first subtleties later turn into abusive behaviour.

Modern dating happens mainly online, where we have anonymity and where it is easy to conceal the red flags. There is a fine line between being appropriately cautious and overly defensive. If we watch out for red flags it can mean that we are distrustful, bitter and too reserved. If we fail to watch out for ourselves, we might fall victim to a narcissist, psychopath, sociopath or any other toxic individual.

If you have ever been in a toxic relationship, the signs might be clear but when you don't know what to watch out for, when you are naive and full of trust and hope, it's easy to be led on, especially by someone who knows how to manipulate you, how to lull your instincts, how to tamper carefully with your thoughts and emotions.

Toxic people are not always mean. They might not even know that they are toxic and draining. It can be because of traumas and the emotional baggage that they carry. There can be excuses and explanations—yet as an adult, you shouldn't need to teach anyone about common courtesy and decency. You shouldn't explain basic notions to anyone, such as attention, reciprocity or patience.

It is possible that it's part of your journey together to adapt to each other, to learn about each other's quirks and weirdness—and it's a great thing. We can learn a lot from the versatility and personal differences. They can show us our boundaries, or they can teach us to be more outgoing, more experimental, more open.

If you feel that something is off, even if you can't put a finger on the reasons, there is a chance that something is really off and it's not just in your mind. It might be just a lack of compatibility, different lifestyles and needs, but you may also be manipulated.

It has become quite common to label someone as narcissistic, mainly because narcissism is an easy and comprehensive label for toxic people—as they usually encompass and showcase more than one toxic trait. The prevalence of narcissism is increasing, yet only 6% of the total population is a real, clinically diagnosed narcissist—with narcissistic personality disorder.

But just because someone is toxic or not a good fit for you, it doesn't mean that they are narcissistic. However, just because someone is not a diagnosed narcissist, it doesn't mean that you are safe from toxicity in your life. Regardless of the label, you need to be aware and watch out for signs of toxicity so you could save yourself from a lot of harm. It is possible to recognise toxic behaviour early on, without getting too emotionally invested in a relationship, where it is already difficult to turn back.

The First Signs of Toxic Behaviour

If you know what you need to watch out for, it is easy to recognize toxic behaviour. But it's much more difficult when you are caught up in the haze of a new relationship. It is easy to let slip behaviours that we wouldn't tolerate any other way. It is easy to forgive someone we are infatuated with. Love makes us irrational; love makes us blind—and this wilful blindness makes us vulnerable.

We see, but we choose not to see.

We ignore the obvious and we come up with excuses.

We choose to see the things that reinforce our beliefs—and when in love, our belief is that we are meant to be together, that the future is bright. We feel invincible and grateful for the person who puts the sparkle in our eyes.

There are things that should feel off. There are things that should raise red flags. There are behaviours that signal danger. It's not easy to pinpoint them, for we don't even want to. But the signs are clear, and the danger is near.

The conversation is never about you

In a relationship, everything should be about reciprocity. The feelings, the favours and the conversations as well. It is quite normal that when you are in a relationship, and you are still in the early phases, you want to get to know the other. You want to know about their lives, their hopes and fears.

With a toxic person, it usually goes to the extreme. As the weeks pass you get to know them, and you become closer with every piece of information. Yet somehow the feeling is not mutual. With a toxic person, after the initial phase when they want to know everything about you (to mirror you later on), their interest fades. You know everything about them, from their first pet to their last workplace conflict—yet they fail to ask you enough questions to get to know you in depth. If you find that the conversation is always about them and you feel that you are but a prop in their show, it's a tell-tale sign that the person you are dating is toxic—or has toxic tendencies.

It feels too easy

It might sound counterintuitive because we are sold on easy love. Romantic comedies and literature paint us a picture where love is easy, and everything goes according to a masterplan. The reason for this is because it goes according to a carefully written plot— it's fiction. I don't believe that fighting and arguments are a sign of a healthy relationship but agreeing about everything is simply unreal.

The beauty of people is their versatility, the different ways of thinking, the different attitudes, the different preferences. It is downright impossible to always like the same things, to always be in sync, to always agree on everything. It is great, but it is usually not true. It either means that the other is subduing themselves and letting go of their own preferences to please you, or it means that you are being manipulated into falling in love.

Love shouldn't be immediately easy. It can't really be, as people are different, and the journey to forming a functioning relationship is a dance where you don't yet know the moves, but you are both willing to learn. It's not about being a perfect match immediately, it's about keeping to choose each other no matter what.

If it feels too easy, it might not be true, and you might be a victim of love-bombing and manipulation from a toxic person.

The world is out to get them

In the first phases of the relationship, it is only right to form a union where the two of you stand together—fighting the odds or the difficulties. But it doesn't have to mean that the whole world is against you.

If your partner is overly worried about the negativity coming from the world, if they feel that everything and everyone is against them—it can be a sign of a toxic individual. Even if it sounds romantic to stand against the world, in reality, the world doesn't care. It is nothing but attention-seeking and responsibility shifting. If someone is overly concerned and blames external circumstances all the time, it's only a matter of time that they will start blaming you for what is happening to them.

A mature individual is a master of their life, fully understanding that consequences follow actions and that there are certain things that they can and should control. Letting go of the responsibility and shifting blame is a red flag.

The ex is crazy

There are crazy exes in the world—it's true. But somehow a toxic individual's exes are *always* crazy. Either for never understanding them, for leaving them, for acting out. Crazy can be real, but it never exists in a vacuum. A crazy ex is rarely a phenomenon of their own making.

If someone cannot talk about their exes in a decent way, you should take it as a sign. Think about it this way: what will stop them badmouthing you in the same way, in case the relationship goes south?

The people we are surrounding ourselves with, speak of us just as much as it speaks of them. It is possible to make bad decisions and choose someone with whom we turn out not to be a great fit. But we still chose them and there had to be something about them that made us stay.

If you don't hear anything positive about any ex, because all of them were selfish, unreliable and crazy, you need to also question your partner. They may be just plain unlucky, or it is them creating the unwelcome environment.

They monopolise your time

It's really nice to be with someone day in and day out—especially in the beginning when you really don't care about anything else. *But healthy relationships leave room for me-time and self-care too.*

If you find that you can't spend any time with your friends or family anymore; if you see that they abandon everything and everyone to be with you— it's not the sign of love, it's the sign of a forming co-dependency, that is extremely unhealthy and toxic.

Isolation is a common tactic of toxic people, as this way they can shape your reality without any external checkpoints. They make you rely on them more than you should rely on anyone, and that makes you vulnerable and exposed to their toxicity.

Monopolising someone's time might sound romantic, but it's not healthy—as your life cannot revolve around one single person.

You feel tired after meeting them

No matter how much you love someone, they can get tiring after a while. Getting away from a loved one, even just for hours or a day can feel great and it can add to the feeling of missing them. It's only natural to be on your own and then be happy about meeting again.

But when your partner makes you feel tired every time you meet them; it might be a sign that something is off. *You deserve to be with people who energise you, not deplete you.* The energy-draining can happen on multiple levels and none of them is too promising. It can be about the drama they create; it can be about the amount of attention they require without reciprocating it; it can be about an imbalance of silence and talking; it can be about too much sex.

The initial period of getting to know each other is to set the boundaries and find out the compromise that works for both of you.

The exhaustion usually happens if the boundaries are constantly stretched—possibly on multiple levels. And if you spend too much time together without having an opportunity to breathe and recharge it can mean that they drain you.

If it happens regularly, it is a sign that they can't respect your boundaries and that's a sign of toxicity.

You get backhanded compliments

A backhanded compliment is any comment that blurs the line between an insult and a compliment. While taking a compliment makes you feel good and receiving an insult angers you or shames you, a backhanded compliment leaves you puzzled and confused. You catch yourself thinking about what they really meant, and you spend a surreal amount of time trying to figure out how you feel.

A great example of a backhanded compliment is: "You look good, *for your age.*" or "You look lovely, *today.*" Was that positive? Do I need to be happy about it? Or is it a put-down? Does it mean that I don't even look good? It's confusing and it's difficult to react, as they can always claim that they meant it as a compliment and it's not up to them that you can't take one.

A toxic person will master the backhanded compliments. They are not downright rude, and they leave a way out of their comment, always the excuse that they meant well. If you feel confused about the compliments you receive you have to start to watch out for other signs, because this kind of passive-aggression is rarely the only sign.

They act differently with you than with others

Do you know the saying that you should judge someone according to how they treat the waiter? You might have the perfect relationship when you are together, yet your partner acts slightly or totally different when you are not alone. It can be either way: they can be overly sweet and way too compliant when there are others present, or they can be rude and impatient—blaming it on external conditions.

When you are with someone, it is common that they will act differently in the bedroom than in a restaurant. But if you see a shift in character that's alarming, you shouldn't sweep your intuition under the rug. Toxic people usually have a mask on that will eventually slip, allowing you to see their real face.

If the difference is too big between what you see when you are alone and when you are not alone, don't ignore the signs.

The Age of Narcissism

He was just staring at his reflection, day in and day out—oblivious to anything else but the beauty of his own face, in the shimmering blueness of the water. He has never seen anything quite like it, no mortal or immortal ever could come close to the perfection of his own mirrored image.

Narcissus, the son of a river god, Cephissus and the nymph, Liriope was warned well in advance. He was said to live to an old age—if he never looked at himself. If only he knew...

He knew his beauty. He knew how mesmerising he appeared to male and female admirers, but not one could touch his heart or invoke his curiosity—he was proud, vain and he rejected them all. He asked them to show their devotion by killing themselves as a sign of love and many of them did. He just laughed and marvelled at the power of his beauty.

A young girl, Echo, fell in love with him, followed him around and professed her everlasting love—but as heartless as he was, he pushed her away, just like all the others. She was nothing to him. So, he condemned her to become nothing. Almost. She wandered the forests, hid among the trees and her broken heart could never be mended. She withered away, faded away from existence, until nothing else was left of her but a mere whisper, an echo, a shadow of something that could have been but never did.

The goddess of vengeance, Nemesis, heard the story of the pretty boy and the devastated girl and cursed Narcissus to fall in love with his own reflection. Narcissus spent his days infatuated with his mirror image in the clear surface of the pond—unable to let go, unable to want to let go. He died there—alone, in his own company, drowning in the everlasting illusion of love and admiration for himself.

A pretty, vain white flower grew where he died—a narcissus.

Wherever you go, you will hear the term narcissistic. It's been thrown around as a buzzword, to describe egotistical, self-centred people—replacing other terms we used to use for self-entitled individuals who were bound to break our hearts.

Are we more narcissistic than ever? Are there more people today displaying narcissistic traits than there used to be? Is it true that the snowflake generation is raised to be narcissistic? Is it about helicopter-parenting and making them believe that they are entitled to have everything?

The Millennial generation has been stereotyped as self-absorbed, self-centred, self-entitled. They are said to be lazy, immature and selfish. They are the snowflake generation, believing that they are one of a kind—overdoing the process of proving it by taking selfies and spending time on social media to gather followers. They refuse to settle for a job, because of the belief that they deserve more than anyone else. Simply put, they are narcissistic. But are they?

The generation, born after 1980 is one of the biggest cohorts in the world—with huge purchasing power and significant impact on everything that happens around the globe. It's not indifferent, whether this generation is bound to be narcissistic— they are too important, too big, too loud, too omnipresent.

In the past ten years, a string of serious debates played out studying the narcissistic personality trait (not the disorder) among members of the GenY.

Narcissism exists on a spectrum, therefore displaying some traits of narcissism doesn't necessarily mean that we have more narcissists among us than we used to have.

While research indicates that the prevalence of narcissistic personality disorder is more common in modern societies than in traditional ones, the lifetime rates of the disorder are reported to be relatively stable for men and women throughout a thirty-year period in which data were collected.

So why do we have so many cases of narcissistic abuse now and why didn't we have them thirty years ago? What is this about?

> *"Every generation worries about the next generation and thinks that it's unique to that generation."* —DR. KALI TRZESNIEWSKI

We know about it more

We don't have more narcissistic people around, we are just more informed, more aware, more educated about the phenomenon. Information travels faster, we have social media, we have 24/7 access to our friends, families and all sorts of informative materials. What used to be just 'battered wives" is now a phenomenon with all its different layers. What used to stay within the family now makes it out and we hear about it more. Women are more empowered, and they don't let themselves be silenced as much as they used to.

Our expectations towards relationships changed and not putting up with maltreatment is one of the beneficial changes that occurred.

We fight patriarchy better

Abuse still happens mainly to women—by men. While there are female abusers and male victims, the gender dynamics of abuse still tap into patriarchy, conservative values and ownership. These days, we fight patriarchy better than we used to. We believe in equality more. Even if there is a lot more work ahead, we have already come a long way. We strive for equal wages, equal rights, equal access to education and resources—as it should be. We believe in empowerment of women. We think that girls are worth just as much as boys.

The strong, independent woman is not labelled as spinster anymore—they are what they are, strong and empowered. There is still a stigma to fight. Still walls to destroy. Still beliefs to get rid of. But this generation—the Millennials—are the first of many that doesn't buy into the patriarchal values of previous generations. They think freely, they act differently.

Selfishness and self-care

Millennials are labelled selfish, when all they do is what they learnt from their parents—to stand up for themselves, to choose themselves and to become independent in thought and action. They believe that the world belongs to them—just like all the previous generations did—but they have different tools to express it. Being digital natives, the Millennial generation is the first to overcome time and distance—to leave a mark—just like every other generation before them wished to.

But selfishness and self-care are two different things. While selfishness is deemed negative—for it might be detrimental to others and society tells us not to harm others; self-care and self-centeredness is a positive trait. In our individualistic society, we need to take care of ourselves. We are left to our own devices. We are pioneers in finding new ways of living, loving and coping. They are not better or worse than anything before, they are just different.

The stereotype-threat

While researchers debate whether the methods, they use to define narcissism are right, another threat emerges: the stereotype threat. Stereotyping a whole generation creates a harmful bias—and it is difficult to fight it individually. When twenty-somethings are expected to have a superiority complex and labelled as immature and lazy, the outer world responds to them differently than it would otherwise.

Negative perception of young people can affect broader trends, like access to jobs and promotions, just as well as their mental health or even their relationships. Another detrimental effect of the bias is that the phenomenon becomes a self-fulfilling prophecy—the more Millennials hear they are lazy, immature and reckless, the more they are prone to believe it and possibly act on it. As if the job market, mental health or our love lives weren't difficult enough to manage without a bias.

It is easy to blame narcissistic Millennials for everything—from ruining the workforce to killing the sanctity of marriage. It is a lot harder to tackle bigger problems in our society that are just revealed by the transparency and honesty that a different world brings.

Our days are not better or worse than what our parents had—it is different. And even if there is narcissism and we are suffering from it, at least we know what we are up against.

Awareness and education are already half the battle won.

Meet the Narcissist

"The lion is most handsome when looking for food." — RUMI

N arcissistic abuse is one of the most heinous things that can happen to someone. It starts with being idealised and idolised, as one is made to believe that they are loveable and appreciated. You are compared to all those who failed before you and it makes you a scarce commodity— someone to love even more.

Then slowly and imperceptibly, cracks appear and the sight you are faced with is far from pretty. You silence your instincts and you turn your head. You refuse to see the red flags, you refuse to hear the sirens blaring, you reject the idea that the perfect love might be imperfect.

When it starts, it's a fairy tale. You are dropped into an ocean of warmth and comfort, perpetually reminded that you are alive and never have been more alive. It's love—and you feel it in every fibre of your being, you radiate happiness and you finally feel that you are seen, heard, loved and desired every moment of every day.

This is the love you have been waiting for and you are falling deeper every minute. You crave this. You deserve this. And they are finally there to give you everything you have ever wanted. You feel appreciated and the situation is perfect—because this is how they make you feel. You are revolving around them—like a planet in the orbit of the sun, enjoying the life that you are given.

You notice the first slip of the mask, yet you choose not to recognise it. You come up with excuses, finding reasoning behind everything they do. They are perfect—and their flaws just make them human, and you love them even more for them.

The mask slips more frequently, and you see yourself finding meaning in it—they are having a bad day, they are stressed, or you were annoying and needy. After all, you are human too.

You buy into your own narrative. True love prevails. Love is not about never having an argument. It is okay to have a bad day. If you love someone, you have to love them at their darkest times too—what would it make of you if you were only a fair-weather lover?

The signs of narcissistic abuse are obvious—when you are looking back. When the puzzle pieces fit, you see everything clearly: how you were used, manipulated, ridiculed and abused. But when you are in it, sucked into the depths of the illusion you want to preserve, it's not so easy to notice the subtle hints.

Narcissistic abuse is a very specific form of abuse. It is a carefully orchestrated string of manipulative events that strips you from your agency, your ability to see clearly, your sense of reality. There are users, losers, abusers, psychopaths and sociopaths out there—hunting for prey, trying to fulfil their needs. There is a whole range of toxic and dangerous individuals who can hurt you – in more ways you could imagine.

The narcissist is different from a toxic person. The narcissist works according to a master plan, where you are but a puppet in their show, where they are in the spotlight, using you to illuminate the way.

The Dark Triad

Narcissism is one of the psychological traits of the Dark Triad. The Dark Triad in psychology refers to the personality traits of Narcissism, Machiavellianism, and Psychopathy. They are called dark for a good reason, as they show malevolent traits. The traits are considered to be distinct, yet more often than not they are overlapping, creating a dangerously manipulative and malignant personality.

Narcissism is characterised by grandiosity, pride, egotism, and a lack of empathy. Machiavellianism is characterised by manipulation and exploitation of others, an absence of morality, and a focus on self-interest and deception. Psychopathy is characterised by continuous anti-social behaviour, impulsivity, selfishness, callousness, and remorselessness.

Personality Disorders

Personality disorders are a class of mental disorders characterised by maladaptive patterns of behaviour, cognition, and inner experience, exhibited across many contexts and deviating from those accepted by the individual's culture. These patterns develop early, are inflexible, and are associated with significant distress or disability. The definitions may vary somewhat, according to source. Official criteria for diagnosing personality disorders are listed in the Diagnostic and Statistical Manual of Mental

Disorders[1] (DSM) and the fifth chapter of the International Classification of Diseases (ICD).

According to DSM-IV and DSM-5 there are three main clusters to categorise personality disorders.

Cluster A (odd or eccentric disorders)

- Paranoid personality disorder: a pattern of irrational suspicion and mistrust of others.
- Schizoid personality disorder: lack of interest and detachment from social relationships, apathy, and restricted emotional expression.
- Schizotypal personality disorder: extreme discomfort interacting socially, with distorted cognition and perceptions.

Cluster B (dramatic, emotional or erratic disorders)

- Antisocial personality disorder: a pervasive disregard for the law and the rights of others.
- Borderline personality disorder: extreme „black and white" thinking, chronic feelings of emptiness, instability in relationships, self-image, identity and behaviour disturbances often leading to self-harm and impulsivity.
- Histrionic personality disorder: pervasive attention-seeking behaviour including inappropriately seductive behaviour and shallow or exaggerated emotions.
- Narcissistic personality disorder: a pervasive pattern of grandiosity, need for admiration, and a lack of empathy.

Cluster C (anxious or fearful disorders)

- Avoidant personality disorder: strong feelings of social inhibition and inadequacy, extreme sensitivity to criticism.
- Dependent personality disorder: pervasive psychological need to be cared for by other people.
- Obsessive-compulsive personality disorder: rigid conformity to rules, perfectionism, and control.

Narcissistic Personality Disorder

It is a Cluster B mental disorder in which people have an exaggerated sense of their own importance, an unhealthy need for attention and admiration. They are characterised by troubled relationships and a complete lack of empathy for others. They are usually charming and irresistible, but behind the mask of confidence and self-esteem, there is a fragile ego, vulnerable to the slightest criticism.

It can stem from various traumas, childhood abuse, neglect and even genetic predisposition. Narcissistic Personality Disorder is a severe, clinically diagnosed form of narcissism.

6.2% of the world's population[2] is diagnosed with it, but narcissism to any degree of toxic extent is way more prevalent than this—and just as with most mental health issues, it is not black or white. Individuals can showcase its traits on a scale.

On the lower end we can find a selfish, entitled individual. On the far end we are talking about Narcissistic Personality Disorder with an emotionally and morally flawed individual who is self-centred, deeply uncaring and cruel, incapable of empathy for others, who hides behind the facade of a charming and attractive person.

According to DSM-5, individuals suffering from narcissistic personality disorder exhibit 5 or more of the following traits, present by early adulthood:
- having an inflated sense of self-importance and entitlement
- needing constant admiration and praise
- expecting special treatment due to perceived superiority
- exaggerating achievements and talents
- reacting negatively to criticism
- being preoccupied with fantasies about power, success, and beauty
- taking advantage of others
- having an inability or unwillingness to recognise the needs and feelings of other people
- behaving in an arrogant manner

Causes

The causes of narcissistic personality disorder are not fully known. Scientists assume that it is consequent to a combination of nature and nurture; of environmental and social, genetic and neurobiological factors.

Possible genetic factors

While it is not scientifically proven, there are some indications—coming from twin studies[3] that there could be a moderate to high probability of NPD being a hereditary personality disorder. There are assumed to be specific genes and genetic interactions that could contribute to someone having or developing narcissistic personality disorder. Basically, it means that if there is a medical history of personality disorders in the family, the condition can be passed on to further generations. It is still undetermined how genetics influence the prevalence of the disorder.

Possible environmental factors

In some cases, pathological narcissism can be a result of distorted emotional attachment to primary caregivers, negatively influencing how the child perceives itself—unimportant, disconnected from others, to family, community or society. Typically, the child starts to believe to be unvalued and unwanted, which can result from both overindulgent and over-controlling parenting.

In Gabbard's Treatments of Psychiatric Disorders[4] the following factors have been identified as contributing factors to developing narcissistic personality disorder:

- An oversensitive temperament at birth.
- Excessive admiration that is never balanced with realistic criticism of the child.
- Excessive praise for good behaviours, or excessive criticism for bad behaviours in childhood.
- Overindulgence and overvaluation by parents, family, and peers.
- Being praised by adults for perceived exceptional physical appearance or abilities.
- Severe abuse (emotional or physical) in childhood.
- Unpredictable or unreliable caregiving by the parents.
- Learning the behaviours of psychological manipulation from parents or peers.

Psychopathology

Researches related to the occurrence of narcissistic personality disorder suggest that structural abnormalities in the brain could also be identified of people with the personality disorder. Studies[5] show lesser volume of grey matter in the left, anterior insular cortex and reduced volume of grey matter in the prefrontal cortex. These two regions, the insular cortex and the prefrontal cortex are associated with empathy and compassion. The neurologic findings suggest that people with narcissistic personality disorder have a damaged capacity for emotional regulation and emotional empathy.

Treatment

"Narcissism is one of the few conditions where the patient is left alone and everyone else is treated." — UNKNOWN

The biggest difficulty with treating narcissistic personality disorder is that narcissists usually fail to recognise that their behaviours are socially unacceptable and problematic—due to their inflated positive self-image, therefore, they rarely seek mental health treatment. It is more common that they seek relief because of external pressure (from partners or family) or to obtain relief of some other mental health issue—depression, substance abuse, bipolar disorder or an eating disorder.

As with many mental health issues, there is no cure, only treatment that would require cooperation and devotion—a will to change. The lack of cooperation and consistent follow-through with any therapy makes it difficult to judge what treatment would work in the long run. Transference-focused therapy, metacognitive therapy and schema therapy are suggested as treatment, along with psycho-pharmaceutical solutions—usually to ease the symptoms of the related disorders, such as depression, anxiety or impulsiveness.

How to Recognise the Narcissist?

Whether someone is a diagnosed narcissist or displaying symptoms without a clinically confirmed diagnosis, there are signs that suggest that you might become a victim of a narcissist and narcissistic abuse. Usually, just as with a clinical definition, they need to display more than just one occurrence of the following traits. A narcissist will eventually display all of them—to some extent.

1. Everything revolves around them

They talk. A lot. And you enjoy it. Finally, someone who can keep up a conversation; there are no awkward silences and you are never bored. They entertain you and make you laugh. They are funny and charming—and the more you know about them the deeper you fall. They dupe you with stories, and everything is a story—they are great storytellers and performers and they adore you for being the best audience.

You listen and praise them, until an instance comes up when you share with them something important and they ignore it, directing the attention towards themselves. You make yourself vulnerable, you open up, you tell them how you feel; perhaps you feel down or insecure only to receive a cliché response or no response at all. It's like they haven't even heard you. The conversation is not about you—ever. It's not about how you feel, not about how your life is, or what you think. *You are not heard, not seen.* You feel invisible.

For the first few times, you can chalk it up to a bad day, a more important story or more significant feelings. But eventually, in a relationship there is no such thing more important than feelings. It's not a competition, it should be equal—both parties being equally heard, seen and respected for their feelings.

If you bring it up, your partner might hear you and listen. They will show you that you are important, calming your fears. But if it keeps happening, they might ridicule you for your insecurity, label you as 'clingy' and accuse you of not paying attention to *them*.

2. You don't feel safe to express your emotions

In a relationship, the most basic need is to feel safe. Even if you don't always talk about your feelings and not every day is about having "the talk", you need to know that when you want to say something, want to bring something up—you are free to do it without repercussions.

In a narcissistic abusive relationship, your feelings don't matter, and it happens often that you get ridiculed for your emotions.

They dismiss your depression, they ignore your anxiety, they get confused and angry at your neediness. You are given a cold shoulder for letting them know that you need more attention and more time or less attention and less control. They stonewall you or they ghost you—only to come back claiming they needed some time out to think and process your needs whether they can live with them.

You are slowly conditioned into not telling them about how you feel. You are taught not to complain about your bad days or your accomplishments.

If you can't express your emotions freely, it might mean that your partner is not mature enough and *you need to talk about how expressing emotions is crucial to a relationship.* With a narcissist it's not about immaturity, it is exactly what it feels like: they don't care about your emotions and they won't pretend that they do. They love it when you express how you feel about them, how much you love them and how much you admire them. Later on, they tolerate your emotions to keep up the appearance, but ultimately, they don't care.

3. You don't recognise yourself

They say that in a good relationship we change—we want to become a better version of ourselves, we work on improvement and to be the best fit for our partner. We do it voluntarily because we want to please our partner. We might choose to be more outgoing, even if we are introverts—to be able to spend more time together, and because compromises are necessary. We might choose to become more experimental and realize that we like some things we haven't liked before.

In a relationship with a narcissist, we slowly change—under their influence. They have subtle ways of telling us how they would want us to be and we change to meet their expectations. Those expectations can be about behaviour or looks or overall values. The change is very subtle, and it doesn't happen overnight. It's almost imperceptible but there are signs.

There are moments of clarity when you don't recognise yourself. You say something cruel about someone else and you are taken back at your own callousness. You look into the mirror and you see a stranger looking back. You forget to call your parents and you get annoyed by the thought of apologizing.

It's not a reflection of the true you—yet it's definitely you changing.

The narcissist is slowly shifting your reality and shapes you, manipulates you into becoming someone else. You might refuse to fit the mould, but they are relentless to change you until you become a different person—less outgoing, less expressive, more dependent on them.

4. You seem to have lost your sense of humour

You have known yourself to be a funny one. With a healthy sense of humour who can take criticism and understand jokes. Yet apparently, you are not fun to be around anymore. It seems that you have lost your sense of humour—or so they say. You are genuinely hurt when your partner ridicules your choice of clothes. For example, your partner may say something demeaning such as *"I didn't know we were going to a Halloween party, you look like a witch."* You don't get their jokes about the shitty dinner—it was a joke, of course, you are a great cook. You don't find it funny that they make fun of your kids—oh, but you see it too; she is really clumsy but in an adorable way. You don't think it's fair to call your mother co-dependent—trailing the words with *"it was just a joke, darling, you know I love that you are close to your mom.'*

Every insult is covered up with a joke. When you call them out on the insult, or you are offended and shocked by something they said—they quickly add that they were just kidding, and you are blamed for not taking the comment with your 'previous' sense of humour.

5. You need to walk on eggshells

Calling them out on what they say and do is the mature thing. You are old enough to know how to communicate assertively—you practised it at your workplace, with previous relationships, with your kids. You know what you want, you know your boundaries and you know how to talk about them in an adult way.

Yet it doesn't work out in your relationship with a narcissist. The first sign is that you realize that they need to win at every situation and every conversation. Even when there is no contradiction from your side, they will still express their opinion being better. They will point out how they are better than you—even though you are not competing with them.

They need to win, and you find it easier not to go against their will, letting it slip. At first, it's very mature of you. But when it becomes regular you start to notice that you watch your words, you start to move out of their way, you start trying to figure out whether they are in a good mood to ask them to do something, or not.

You are walking on eggshells—and you are protecting their ego, you care for their workload, you defend their fragility—even if it's not in your best interest.

6. You find yourself in déjà vu conversations

A normal relationship consists of repetitive situations—you are getting into an everyday routine and it's only fair that you have the same conversation topics regularly. Topics usually involve work, children, friends and family.

With a narcissist, it's usually about how they see the world—with a couple of agreements from you injected into their viewpoint. But even within the constant hum of your partner singing their own songs of praise or complaining about their lives, you will find yourself hearing the same stories again and again.

They don't pay enough attention to keep up a normal conversation and they don't care about being repetitive. They are happy to tell you about their biggest romantic achievement, their star promotion ten years ago, their perfect child (who is definitely not yours).

They use word salad against you to confuse you. Word salad is a circular conversation of repeating the same 2–3 basic thoughts phrased differently for appearance. They circle back and forth from the original subject and in a few minutes, you lose track of what the initial starting point was.

They use this technique in arguments and when you call them out. They will quickly direct the conversation back to a topic where they were still great, why they should be appreciated, or how you are mistaken or too sensitive.

7. The double standards are killing you

The boundaries for the narcissist are very vague. They believe that they are superior to everyone else and the rules don't apply to them. This means that those who follow the rules—including you—may be stupid and a pushover. This means that they are free to break the rules—and they do it often.

Whatever the topic is, they are above the rest of us, so those that apply to us will never apply to them. They will tell you to work harder to get your promotion yet get extremely annoyed if you suggest that the reason for them not being promoted was that they had just started a new job. They will tell you to speak less and be less of a know-it-all yet will go to extreme lengths to tell every one of your friends about how they should live their lives. They will never allow you to express your emotions yet will demand you to listen to them when they want to express theirs.

Double standards exist everywhere, and it is difficult to fight them, but when the allegedly same values get tweaked and twisted within your relationship, and you are not allowed the same *privileges* as them, it's an instant red flag.

8. They don't take no for an answer

They say that the best test to spot a narcissist is to tell them no. They say that they will spiral into a rage and this is how you will know it. It would be great to spot them this easily, but it's not that black and white. They are smarter than this.

They don't take no for an answer and it manifests in different ways. At first, it's incredibly flattering when they don't take no for an answer. When you try to cancel on them and they beg you to just meet them for five minutes, they just want to see you and hold you—and you give in. After all, who doesn't want to be loved that much—and they win. Then later when you try to establish boundaries, they agree to them—and then they ignore it. They don't even take it as a no, boundaries are neglected, and they don't care about rules.

If it starts to get out of hand and you ask for some me-time—they might stonewall you, ghost you and punish you with their absence. Then coming back, they gaslight you that it was you who wanted them to be gone, causing you major guilt and self-doubt.

The end game is that you are not one to make decisions — they are. The relationship is on their terms. It is important to notice that the ghosting and stonewalling only happens when you are sufficiently reeled in and they are sure that it will hurt you. And that is the ultimate goal of a narcissist; in that any interaction will benefit them.

9. You can't count on them

Speaking of saying no and making decisions—they are the ones to make decisions. It is perfectly okay in a relationship if something comes up and one needs to cancel, or plans need to be adjusted. But it's not okay if that one is always them.

Within a relationship with a narcissist, you will learn quickly that you are not entitled to their time, while they are entitled to yours. You need to report about your whereabouts, plans and availability—which you take as a sign of caring. *It's not caring, it's control.*

But when you ask to know what their plans are, they become distant and defensive, they call you clingy and needy. They keep stringing you along and in loads of cases, they cancel on you at the very last minute.

If you realize that you can't count on them, they don't treat your time and attention as importantly as you should treat theirs, it's a sign that they are entitled and selfish. If it happens in a normal relationship, you are free to bring it up, express your concern and work towards a solution. Perhaps clearer communication is needed, maybe earlier planning is required—maybe it can be sorted out with a little more attention.

The narcissist will not want to work it out, as your time and your life is not important enough to change their ways about their own time and their own life.

10. You get your apology, but it doesn't mean a thing

There is great power in apologising. Sometimes apologising means that you are the bigger person, and you care enough about the other to suppress your ego. It takes a lot to tell someone that you were wrong—and those who can apologize are worthwhile people. Except for the narcissist.

The point of an apology is twofold:

1. admitting your fault and the fact that it is possible to make a mistake and

2. recognising a behaviour that is not to be repeated later on.

No one likes to apologise, and it is better trying to act in a way that you don't need to apologise for your behaviour.

The narcissist is very good at apologising. It is their way of solving a conflict. They will put on a show and display genuine guilt and remorse to make you believe that they are sorry for what they have said or what they have done. It's all honourable—until you realize that their apology is empty and weightless, and they have zero intention to change their behaviour. They apologise and they do the same thing a day later.

If you see that your partner is willing to apologise a little too quickly—it might not be a bad sign. They might love you and this is their way of expressing their love. But if no change can be observed in the faulty behaviour then the apology is meaningless, *and you might be dating a narcissist.*

3. NARCISSISTIC ABUSE

Abuse Is Gradual

I asked myself and others multiple times. Why didn't I notice what was going on? Why didn't I adhere to my boundaries? Why did I stay? Why didn't I leave?

Three important facets of abuse:

1. Victim blaming is a terrible and common phenomenon—and it's so prevalent that even the victims blame themselves for not having known better.

2. Abuse is always the abuser's fault.

3. Abuse isn't always immediate.

We'll come back to victim blaming in detail later, but first, we will address why it is difficult to recognise abuse. Abuse may not be immediate. It can be slow, imperceptible and gradual.

If your date calls you shames you on your first encounter, you won't see them again. If your boyfriend hits you or if rape is involved, you would report them; you run in the other direction without ever looking back.

But abuse may be less obvious at first; it mainly happens in close relationships, where love and care suppress the signs. The events seem so unlikely that you find an explanation for even the most heinous of acts.

Abuse happens on many levels—and can unfold unnoticeably, so that when you suddenly realize it, you will need to admit it to yourself that it has been ongoing from the beginning—only there was no opportunity for you to identify it.

Just Words...

The verbal abuse is usually the first to start. Narcissists have a tendency of love-bombing, to idealise, discard, devalue their victims. First and foremost, they will use words to do that. They shower you with their attention to build themselves up as the perfect partner, the better to gain your trust, affection and, ultimately, adoration. It is very important for them to do it quickly and effectively as they know that once the partner sees through their façade, the relationship may self-destruct. Once they have convinced you of how good the two of you are together, how perfect everything is, that you are soulmates, and once they have secured your affection they will start to push your limits, push you away, just to prove how worthless you are to them. They devalue and discard you, only to start over with love-bombing, when the relationship starts to fall apart.

For me it was the slowest possible build-up. Commenting on my work, on the words that I used, even making funny remarks about my cooking. I cooked something for him, and he just loved it. He praised me for it for days, claiming that he's never had anything that delicious and that solely for that reason, he should marry me immediately. I laughed it off, but it made me very proud. And happy. The next time I made the exact same dish in a week because he loved it so much, it was just "not as good". He was apologetic about putting it down, and he still said it was very tasty, but you know "something is missing", maybe the salt or the cheese was more fresh the other day, or something else. And I felt defeated. I put all my effort and love into it, and he convinced me that I was at fault. He even said it was not my fault and how much he appreciates it. This is how it started. Very slowly, very subtly. I did not notice how the temperature had changed, all I realized was that I woke up one day, feeling miserable, broken and sad all the time. The verbal abuse slowly got worse. From slight put-downs, it turned into tasteless jokes and insults at first, then it turned into name calling. I was called a slut, a whore, a worthless piece of meat, just to name a few insults. This came from the man who professed to love me.

Alienation

Alienation is another common tactic of narcissists. First, they want your full attention, and they work for it too. It feels great; unconditional, and undisturbed. 'It's just us against the world' mentality. 'They are all just jealous of what we have, this once-in-a-lifetime earth-shattering love' mentality. It feels good, overwhelming but still good. It is gradually changing into controlling behaviour, where if you spend time with anyone else—your kids, your family, your friends, even your colleagues at work—it becomes insulting for them, proof that you don't love them anymore. So, the next step is to remove everyone from your environment. By demanding full attention, by dragging down everyone, by making comparisons between you and them (how much better you are than your friend, brother or mother, how much smarter you are than all your colleagues, how perfect of a mother you are to raise individual kids, so you should just let them play on their own, etc.).

You might tell your friends about the first fight and the first happy romantic getaway that follows, but after the 5th one in rapid succession it stops being reasonable and comprehensible—and to save face, it is better not to complain about your own choice. Plus, there is a huge element of cognitive dissonance, too.

I realized that I didn't talk to my friends because there was just nothing to say anymore. I couldn't tell them how happy I was with him, because it was not true anymore. And I couldn't tell them how miserable I was with my partner, because I wanted it to work and I couldn't admit it to anyone that this was not a dream, this was a nightmare. I was failing at work, as my mind was constantly occupied by the things that were happening at home. I was clever enough to hide my failures and somehow managed to deliver my responsibilities, but deep down I knew that I wasn't even giving it half of my potential. I was terrified when my friends and family would notice it.

And I was ashamed. Ashamed of being sad when I should be happy and in love, ashamed to admit that I was called a whore and I didn't kick him out, but I wanted to comfort him. Ashamed because I thought that it was my fault that he dropped the coffee mug and I didn't catch it, so it stained his trousers.

I had lucid moments when I called him out on his behaviour, threatened to kick him out if he ever spoke to me that way. He promised to do everything, broke down in tears, blamed the alcohol, his boss, the weather — or in some cases he blamed me. If I hadn't dressed so provocatively then he wouldn't have become jealous. And he made me feel ashamed for dressing up, even for work.

Abusing Sexuality

Narcissists use sexuality as a way to bond love and sex together. Sex is always about love; love is always manifested in sex. It's a slow but steady process, to form an undistinguishable association between the two. And what can go wrong if it's done out of love? *Everything.* It is about power and manipulation, it is about obsessing over his own sexual performance, it is on the borderline of consent or just slightly out of it, it is always on his terms and his terms only. It is about stretching boundaries and using everything you ever say or do against you, using your own pleasure and desire to ridicule you and hurt you in the most humiliating way possible.

I did not enter in a relationship that started out with rape. It just got there. We had an amazing sex life. We connected very early on and with time passing it just got better and better to the point of euphoria. And as it happens in new relationships, we were together frequently. That was very satisfying at first. I had my best orgasms and sometimes more than enough of it, to the point of such exhaustion that I could barely get up the next day. It was good — at first. And then it wasn't. I was too tired to have sex three times a night. And if I wasn't up for it, the jealousy and name calling started. "You were with someone else, that's why you don't want it with me?"

Bruises and Frozen Peas

Physical and sexual abuse is about power and the possibility of hurting the other—just because they

84

can. It is a gradually escalating phenomenon, as part of the abuse cycle, where the build-up of the tension, the abuse and the honeymoon phases follow each other in a vicious, never-ending cycle.

The first blow was not a blow. He just pushed me and squeezed my arm a little too strong, so it left a mark. Then he hit me. And I still stayed. He went to therapy, started to take medications, talked to a therapist as well. He claimed that he wanted to change. Little did I know that he never wanted to change. It was such a comfortable life for him, with no responsibility nor consequence whatsoever. And at this point, I already had our baby. There was more at stake, not just me. I already knew how to lock myself in the room without installing a lock. How to make good use of frozen peas to make bruises go away before they even formed. I knew which foundation can cover my black eye so that no one sees it. I knew what herbal ointments help to heal the black and blue spots quicker and I had a load of them in my medicine cabinet. Despite the summer I was wearing long sleeved t-shirts, baggy enough not to touch my skin and to cover my wounds.

The Vicious Circle of Abuse

The cycle of abuse concept comes from domestic violence prevention programs—and it originates from Lenore E. Walker, who interviewed 1.500 women who had been subject to domestic violence. She found a common pattern of abuse among the majority of respondents and she called this the **'cycle of abuse'**. Initially, it was called 'the battering cycle' and 'battered woman syndrome' before it was renamed a more comprehensive term— for abuse doesn't only happen to women and doesn't always lead to physical abuse.

The recognised patterns are still valid—even though there have been more elaborate and detailed versions of it, the main principles still apply. Its cyclical nature refers to the never-ending dynamics—

ending only when the conflict is stopped—usually due to some intervention or the survivor leaving the relationship.

The cycles can occur repeatedly—and completing them can take anywhere from days to years. It is also observed that the length of the cycle usually decreases over time, eventually skipping the calm stages—displaying the constant negative cycle.

Abuse Cycle Phases

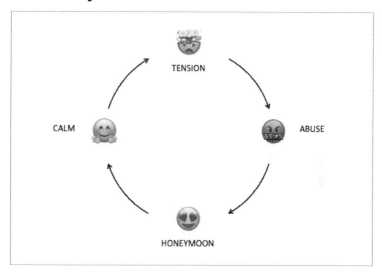

Tension building

Within a relationship the tension starts building from the impacts of daily life—marital issues, conflicts over money or children, misunderstandings. Illness, financial problems, unemployment or external events can contribute to it—as well as mental instability and substances.

The victims might want to prevent the cycle from moving forward by becoming compliant and obedient or they might even trigger it, so they can prepare for it instead of being caught off-guard or for it to be over with it.

Violence

This stage is about the actual violence—that is usually with the objective to dominate the victim and exert power over them. It could be verbal, psychological or physical abuse—depending on the nature of the abuser.

This stage releases the tension and once it's over it will pass onto the next phase (the cycle can skip the next two phases).

Honeymoon

The abuser—after the tension is gone—may start to feel guilty or remorseful about their actions. They usually also become afraid of repercussions, such as the victim leaving them or calling the police.

The victim might feel they triggered their partner, so they take the responsibility and forgive the abuser as they once more turn into someone charming and caring. Displays of affection, gifts and promises and reignited passion are typical features of the honeymoon phase. The abuser might threaten with suicide or self-harm and promise to change—to keep the relationship going.

The honeymoon phase gives hope to the victims and usually the abusers are convincing enough so victims stay in the hope of keeping together the relationship.

Calm

During the phase of calmness, the usual—nice—life returns, and it prolongs the honeymoon phase, full of promises and hope. The abuser usually agrees to whatever it takes to keep going: counselling, giving up substances and apologies and forgiveness are regular.

This intermittent reinforcement makes the relationship even more desirable—for it shows that the good times are possible, and the bad times don't last.

The cyclical nature of the abuse calls for the tension building after a period of calm. The cycle might get shorter, the apologies less sincere. Over time the cycle leads to loss of love and contempt and might result in the partners separation or divorce or in extreme cases, homicide.

Narcissistic Abuse Cycle

The narcissistic abuse is slightly different, but just as cyclical. The end phases of the cycle might change, for the narcissist is unwilling to admit fault—they won't even pretend it, unless they really have to.

In a narcissistic abusive situation, the abuse is followed by the narcissist playing the victim and shifting the blame to the partner.

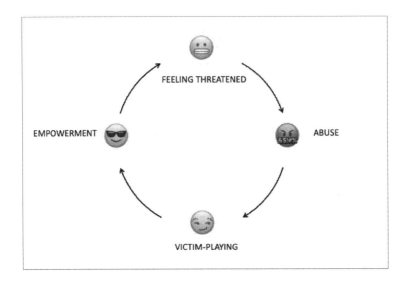

Feeling threatened

Similarly, as in a regular abuse cycle, the narcissist is distressed by daily events. They feel that their ego is threatened—it could be rejection, disapproval, embarrassment. They can feel jealous of others' successes or they might feel that their needs are not met—coming from perceived abandonment, neglect or disrespect. It is usually going back to the same type of threat—depending on the innermost fears of the narcissist.

The abused feels the tension and they walk on eggshells to avoid the abuse—or to slow down the process. The abused trying to avoid triggering the narcissist might work, but it eventually moves to the next phase despite any effort—because it is a power play.

Abuse

The narcissist starts some kind of abusive behaviour—it can be anything, verbal, mental, emotional, financial or physical abuse. It is tailored to the abused—the narcissist is expert at finding the victim's weak spots and using everything they have ever said or done against them. It can last a few seconds or even hours and days.

The provocative nature of narcissistic abuse will eventually get the victim to fight back defending their words, actions or their peace of mind. This is when the next phase begins.

Victim-playing

When the abused can't take the abuse anymore they fight back to defend themselves and *it's time for the narcissist to play the victim*. The abuser claims that the victim deliberately abuses them—forgetting the initial abuse coming from them.

The narcissist completely buys into their own narrative, and believe that they are the actual victim. As convincing as they usually are, the real victim starts to feel remorse and tries to ease the tension by giving in, apologising and complying fully even with the most impossible requests.

The situation temporarily gets better—and both the narcissist and the victim feel they have resolved the issue. Displays of love and affection occur—as long as it's the victim who is making the compromise and the narcissist doesn't need to change.

Empowerment

Once the narcissist sees that once again the victim has been defeated, they feel empowered and their ego is stroked enough to feel superior and right. With giving in to the power play, the victim inadvertently contributes to the repetition of the cycle—as it is too easy to manipulate them.

The victim feels confused, but the narcissist feels great from winning another battle that they had created.

As their ego is too fragile and they are easy to upset the empowerment can quickly turn into feeling threatened, again. No matter how much the victim tries to avoid it by walking on eggshells and complying with their requests, the narcissist is near-impossible to please, so the cycle continues.

And so the cycle continues.

It is characterised by intermittent reinforcement, to make it even more powerful and devastating.

Intermittent Reinforcement

In behaviourism, the term intermittent reinforcement refers to a phenomenon in which the reward or punishment is not administered consistently, but according to a random schedule. Its opposite, continuous reinforcement means that every time a certain action is performed there is a reward or punishment for it.

Interestingly, there is an increased likelihood of achieving the expected conditioning with intermittent reinforcement than with continuous reinforcement—for the unpredictable and random reward fires up a euphoric response in the brain.

Gambling is a great example of intermittent reinforcement. You can't win every time, or you don't win the same amount—it is unpredictable and uncertain, which gives a bigger chemical reward when the random win occurs. In some circumstances it can lead to an addiction.

This random schedule is what narcissists use to condition their victims with a constant hot and cold, push and pull behaviour—you don't know when it is coming, be it about the abuse or the unexpected display of affection.

The uncertainty plays a huge role in getting addicted to the other—and it also reinforces trauma bonding. You would assume that we cling to stable and predictable situations, but science proves otherwise. There is an inexplicable pull towards the things that we can't have—especially when it comes to romantic partners.

But why do we want what we can't have?

We are establishing our own dynamics of being inferior

When it comes to romantic and sexual attraction, regardless of what we expect from the other person, we tend to overestimate their qualities. At the first moments of meeting, when we subconsciously decide about them, we size them up. If we have chemistry, we immediately assign more value to them than they deserve. Just because we are attracted to them with all of our senses, we are getting a hormone cocktail that waves goodbye to our rational minds. We see, we hear, we smell, we touch, and if it comes to that, we taste. The stronger the chemistry, the worse our capability is for evaluating them properly.

If the chemistry or later the attraction stays strong enough, without really knowing them, we start to overvalue them and undervalue ourselves. It doesn't matter if we see them in a distorted reality, the less we know about them, the more gaps there are to fill with our imagination.

And sometimes even a person with an average level of self-esteem will start degrading themselves to keep up the gap between the overvalued romantic interest and them. It is because of cognitive dissonance when we are trying to post-rationalise our decisions to stay sane—but in this case, it works against us.

The myth of unavailability

We live in a busy world, and we live hectic lives. We are spreading ourselves thin, and we romanticise unavailability and busyness. If someone appears unavailable or distant, giving the impression that they are involved and needed, we place more perceived value on them and we tend to appreciate people who respond less or reciprocate our initiations less. We think that someone's unavailability is correlating with their popularity, and we believe they must really be worth it since they are in such high demand.

Someone's perceived busyness makes them look like scarce resources and their value increases. It results in us thinking they must be spending time with others, that lowers our self-esteem even more; and we are even more grateful for the tiny amounts of attention they are showing, as if it was a great sacrifice from their side.

Someone's lack of response shouldn't imply a higher value, as it is usually a sign of disinterest, lack of communication skills or just plain rudeness.

Unfortunately, it is difficult to walk away, because of the intermittent reinforcement their infrequent appearances cause. When we like someone, our brain releases dopamine to make us feel good whenever they message or talk to us. We get addicted to the hormone rush and start to go after our next dose. The intermittent attention strengthens our craving and makes the relief even more powerful, thus making us even more addicted.

As Erika Ettin, founder of A Little Nudge dating website, says: "Our brains love unpredictability because the highs are higher than if we got the desired reward all the time. This is why breadcrumbing has sadly entered our lexicon recently."

Breadcrumbing is when someone texts or calls on a sporadic basis, generally because they know you will respond. They will seem to be pursuing you, but in reality, have no intention of being tied down to a relationship. They just like leaving you breadcrumbs, like a trail in Hansel and Gretel, to string you along. We let them treat us this way just to get our even higher dopamine rush anytime they unexpectedly appear.

The erotic equation

The term erotic equation was coined by Jack Morin in his book, "The Erotic Mind." Central to Morin's understanding of sexual passion is what he calls "The Erotic Equation": attraction plus obstacles equal excitement. He says that although most couples envision a harmonious love life, sexual arousal thrives upon conflict and "the dark side of lust." He suggests that sex is paradoxical, which in his equation means full of obstacles. He says a foundational, healthy approach to sex involves "embracing the paradoxical perspective."

According to Morin, the four cornerstones of eroticism are longing, prohibition, power and ambivalence. Explaining our attraction to unavailable people, we get to some factors that show that longing and anticipation are strengthened by prohibitions and obstacles and also by ambivalence.

This means the more we aren't supposed to have something or someone, and the more conflicted we feel about our own emotions—the higher the excitement and the arousal becomes. And the greater our desire is, the greater satisfaction comes from getting it; even to some extent.

We all say that we crave stability, but studies show differently.

According to a study, attractive potential partners were described as having either low, intermediate, or high availability. When asked who they would most like to date and what kind of restaurant they'd take that person to, participants tended to choose the low availability target and, they decided to take them to the fanciest restaurant, too.

In another study, participants were told that an attractive person liked them a lot, liked them an average amount, or liked them at an unknown level. Participants then rated how attracted they were to the target. Not surprisingly, people were drawn to the prospect who liked them a lot over the prospect who liked them an average amount. However, they were actually most attracted to the prospect who liked them an unknown amount!

Uncertainty works on a few levels here. On the one hand, being uncertain about someone else's feelings can be seen as an obstacle to pursuing something with them (and attraction plus obstacle means excitement). However, uncertainty could also create a sense of mystery that draws you in, further increasing excitement.

Intermittent Reinforcement as an Abusive Tool

It's just a phone call that isn't made when promised. Just a date cancelled or something important postponed. It's a seemingly innocent flirty comment to the waitress, then denial of it. It's just not being in the mood for sex—refusing all initiations for a full week. It's a promise to explain their behaviour—and then it's forgotten for good.

It starts slow and with such small things that we don't even recognise. It feels great when they finally text and call—so we don't even want to go into an argument about the one time that it was missing. We don't want to appear jealous for no reason—so we let the flirting go and we tell ourselves that we have to work on our self-esteem so that the irrational shouldn't interfere with a perfect relationship. We admit that it is fine not to want sex all the time and consent is important; we wouldn't want to take it away from anyone. And as the narcissist manipulatively withdraws sex, complications arise about consent and want, typically the victim must respect the narcissist so that things don't get worse.

But then it gets worse. The missing text turns into the silent treatment—when they abandon us for days without a word. The flirting turns into unfair comparisons to other women—our age, weight, body, behaviour are criticised. Our quirks, that they used to love, become a reason for mocking. That cute dance they loved becomes ridiculous and shameful. The way we dress becomes tasteless, slutty or boring.

They stonewall us—and then they come back, denying it all. They compare us to others and then they call us too 'sensitive'. They listen to our complaints and then they call us clingy. They pay us backhanded compliments. *"I love how clingy you are."* *"I never liked blondes and you are not my type at all, but I am so attracted to you." "You really dress nice, considering your age."* They provoke us to the extent of an emotional meltdown and then ridicule us for it—we should just pull it together, finally.

But then they show up the next day, like nothing happened—they bring flowers and take us out for a date, showering us with love, affection and show us passion we haven't yet seen. They make us forget that we were hurt, because they are finally back, the charming, loving, incredible person we feel for is back. And heaven is back too, until they decide to take it away again. And that they will do. Soon.

The Empath Meets The Narcissist

When you look back, it seems so clear. But when you are caught up in it, it's very difficult to see the reality for what it is. I kept asking myself why it happened? Why did I invite this whole experience? What should I have done differently? Was I at fault? Why did he choose me? What is it about me that lures a toxic person and promises them that they will get their fix?

I didn't see it coming, because I wanted something extraordinary. It was everything I have ever wanted, everything I have ever wished for, and so many things I have never even dreamt to ask for. It was love, pure and raw and earthmoving love that changes you and changes how you see the world. I loved so fiercely and wildly that I failed to see that behind the mask of this bird with a broken wing, whom I wanted to save so much, lied a vulture who was hungry to devour my energy and soul.

When it was over, and my heart was shattered and I couldn't even bother to try to pick up the pieces, the worst was yet to come: the realisation that this love only existed in my mind, and what I believed to be the greatest love on earth was nothing but fuelling someone's unrequited self-love.

> *"I thought narcissism was about self-love till someone told me there is a flip side to it. It is actually drearier than self-love; it is unrequited self-love." — EMILY LEVINE*

It wasn't about me. But there is an explanation why it happened to me.

I am an empath. And I fell in love with a narcissist. And in a way, he fell in love with me, too. But this way was a destructive, fatal way to fall in love.

In a disproportionate number of cases empaths will find themselves involved with a narcissist, and as impossible as their attraction seems, these completely opposite personalities are drawn to each other like moths to a flame, their collision being fatal and inevitable—for the empath. What is behind these dynamics? Let's take a look at the empath. Then let's explore the seemingly inexplicable attraction to a narcissist.

Who is the Empath?

Empaths are those highly sensitive individuals who are uniquely tuned in to the emotions of people surrounding them, with the ability to sense what others are thinking and feeling. They are sensitive, kind, nurturing, big-hearted and generous. They are intuitive and have exceptionally high emotional intelligence. They are the perfect friends, the ones who will always be there for you, who will always listen, who will always care.

However, these qualities can be hard on the empaths themselves. They are feeling what others are feeling, they feel the suffering, they take on the pain, anxiety or anger of their friends and loved ones. They have a hard time with setting healthy boundaries for themselves, they are bad at saying "no", and they are loyal to a fault, often placing others' needs before their own.

One possible scientific explanation for why empaths are so receptive is the discovery of mirror neurons. We all have a set of neurons in our brains that fire up whenever we witness something that another person feels or experiences. These mirror neurons help us to learn through imitation. When we are young, for example, we learn to speak and behave through the imitation of our parents and siblings. As we age, the number of mirror neurons slowly decrease as their presence is needed most for our survival through growth. Not with the empaths who keep their mirror neurons active well into their adult lives.

The discovery of mirror neurons reveals why empaths feel extreme disgust, pain, and horror when watching acts of violence. Mirror neurons also hint at why empaths carry so much emotional deadweight from others.

The Attraction

It doesn't seem to make sense that two such people: the narcissist and empath, would be even remotely attracted to each other. Yet it still happens.

Why is the narcissist attracted to the empath?

It is easy to understand from the narcissist point of view why he finds the empath so attractive: the empath is everything that they will never become—kind, caring, supportive, stable. The empath listens, the empath understands, the empath is emotionally available. This is heaven for the narcissist. It's like winning the lottery: an empath has a lot of love, they care, they want to help, they want to give—because this is what makes them happy. And this is what the narcissist wants: to be loved, to be cared for, to be helped, to take and take. The void in them is so crippling that they need to go at extreme lengths to fill it.

The attraction is about filling the void.

But why is the empath attracted to the narcissist?

There are two layers to this:

1. The narcissist, in the beginning, is caring, funny and irresistible, they have an overwhelming charm—they have a powerful vibe. They are very intense—on every level. They showcase their own irresistibility; their objective is selling themselves and how wonderful they are and revealing how wonderful the empath is.

2. The empath senses some kind of disturbance, *there is something off*—it's like when you can't tune to a radio station and beyond the music, you hear crackling and white noise. The empath sees a challenge here: they *need* to figure this one out. The narcissist is very good at appearing helpless, lost and broken—and this is an open invitation for the empath. Like a flashing neon sign: 'come and help me', 'come and save me.' The narcissist is openly admitting how wounded they are, and this is not an act, they really are broken inside. This triggers the empath to get into *saviour mode*. The narcissist is adept at making the empath believe they are the only one who can help them, or that they already have.

The attraction is about wanting to save them

It is the fatal blind spot of the empath, because the narcissist cannot be helped and more importantly, they don't want help. It is a dangerously co-dependent relationship which revolves around superficially fulfilling the needs of only one person who can be neither satisfied nor happy. The narcissist is like a leaky bucket: no matter how much you pour into it, it never fills up, nothing is enough.

The narcissist cannot and will not change. They are not capable of the type of emotion, empathy and compassion that is needed to become a fair, loving, and caring partner—and they can never learn. They cannot learn how to be a "real" person. This ability is learned in the first few years of life. By the time the empath meets the narcissist, it is already far too late. They cannot be helped.

It's hard to avoid the charisma of the narcissist, and sometimes even hard to spot them; they're social chameleons. They know exactly what to say and do to make you feel however they want you to feel.

What To Do, If You Are An Empath?

If you're an empath, you need to develop a strong sense of self, to be able to fend off people who would feed off you and take you for granted. You need to understand that having boundaries is not rude, but necessary; that sacrificing yourself will not bring you happiness; and that co-dependency is not a healthy type of attachment.

Since it is unrealistic to expect that the narcissist will ever recognise their problems, it is up to the empath to recognise the situation and resolve it. The first thing that one must realize is that the only way to resolve the situation is to get out of it. That is a very hard truth to face. It is terrible to believe and admit that you have wasted months, years or even decades of your life on someone who doesn't care or appreciate it at all. This is especially hard when dealing with a narcissist who swears this is not the case.

Don't take responsibility for other people's hurt

You need to remind yourself constantly that you have one responsibility: your own life and happiness. You feel their pain, you feel their struggle and you want to help, but there is only so much you can do. You can help and guide them, you can be there for them, but at the end of the day you can only help someone who is willing to help themselves too. Their hurt and their healing are not in your hands. You need to recognise that there are a lot of people who don't want to be fixed because being in pain or in misery is safe and comfortable, no matter what.

Set clear boundaries

You need to learn to set clear boundaries. You need to identify the fine line where you are being helpful and where it is sucking the life out of you. You need to learn to be selfish—in the most positive sense of the word. You need to learn to say no if something doesn't fit your schedule, your own needs, your expectations. Saying no is not being rude, it's teaching others about your needs and boundaries, it is about telling them how to treat you—and in case they take it the wrong way, the problem lies with them, not you. You are entitled to say no to others who are using you or your help or time or energy—without getting anything in return.

Trust your instincts

The weirdest thing about empaths is that they have exceptional capabilities in terms of gut feelings. They sense other people, they sense situations—yet they are quick to ignore red flags when it comes to helping others. The empath usually knows that there is something off with the narcissist, they see it and feel it. But the discomfort of the blurry picture is washed away by their wish to help.

The empath needs to trust their instinct a lot more. They need to give themselves more credit for their own feelings and suspicions. Think back on it: how many times did your gut feeling fail you? How many times did you need to convince yourself to do something against your instinct, because you thought that was expected of you—to be kind and nice and caring to a fault. Your instincts are there for a very good reason. It is to save you—even from yourself. Listen to it. Practice it, tune in to yourself, and believe in yourself—no second-guessing, you are way better than that!

Watch out for red flags

When it comes to others' lives, you know what to watch out for. When you need to give advice to your friends, there is no one else who could guide them in a more insightful and spot-on way but you. Remind yourself, that the red flags are the same for you as well. You can't decide to not see them, just because they are so close that they are covering everything else from your vision. You need to take one step back and observe your own life from a distance—use your highly developed empathy skills, and ask yourself what would you suggest if it wasn't you, but a friend? You would watch out for them. Try to protect them. Try to save them from any harm.

Be your own best friend and listen to your invaluable advice.

Learn to walk away

The hardest part is to walk away from toxic situations. And it is not because of your ego or dignity. *It is because you feel that you have failed.* You failed to help them, you failed to save them, you failed to keep your promises. Walking away is the second-best thing you can do. The first is not walking in such a situation—but for that, you need to learn a lot, to work on your self-esteem and your boundaries. You need to know that your worth is not linked to your capability of helping and saving others. Your gift is your compassion, not your unilateral struggle to save someone who refuses to be saved anyway.

Why Would Anyone Fall
For a Narcissist?

You would think that mature adults are not easy to be conned into a relationship—but think again. When you don't know who you are facing, when you trust that people are inherently good, when you don't hold back with your emotions—you are being true to yourself.

And an empowered, strong, independent person can be very attractive. They have everything that the narcissist might need. And the narcissist has the toolset to exploit your naïveté and abuse your trust in ways you can't even imagine.

They Choose You Because You Meet Their Criteria

Narcissists have exquisite radar to spot individuals who will be most likely to fall for them. It is quite usual that their victims are the complete opposite of them—as in they are capable of filling the void for their narcissistic character in every sense.

While there are no criteria for them in terms of looks or social status, they will usually go for someone caring, loving and full of empathy—the exact features that they lack.

It seems very unlikely that they can con an empathetic, smart individual—though they possess all the skills to capitalise on the vulnerable sides of an empath.

An empathetic person is everything that a narcissist will never become—kind, caring, supportive, stable. Narcissists look for someone who listens, understands, and who is emotionally available. Empathetic people have a lot of love, and they care, they want to help, they want to give—because this is what makes them happy and it's who they are.

And this is precisely what the Narcissist wants: to be loved, to be cared for, to be helped, and to *take*.

They Will Mirror You

It is assumed that someone with narcissistic personality disorder or an individual not meeting the clinical criteria, but situated higher up on the scale, wouldn't have a stable personality. Still, they are very good at adapting to others' behaviour—at least some of the time.

It is proven that when we enter a romantic relationship, we are going for the familiarity, the qualities that we already know, and features that we already possess.

Mirroring is an excellent technique to win the trust of your partner. Mirroring is a negotiation and sales technique that is widely used by experts, and it involves body language, meta-communication and use of words. Even therapists use it as an ice breaker, using your words and your expressions to make you feel understood and more at ease.

Narcissists use our natural need for connection by mimicking our traits and thus making us fall for our own reflection. It is not unheard of that the early stages of a narcissistic relationship are full of '*Aha!*' moments when we discover that we have so many things in common.

We like the same food, the same music, and we want to go out or stay at home to equal measures. There are never arguments, as they are just like us. This is not coincidental—they are observing us, they pay attention, and they respond to our character by showing very similar traits. It feels like a match made in heaven. We are soulmates with the same values, same likes and dislikes. *Only it's not true.* They do everything to reel us in, and the easiest way is if we are so similar that we are clearly meant to be.

They Will Love-Bomb You

The beginning of a relationship is one of its best parts—it's intense, it's reassuring, and it holds just the right amount of intermittent reinforcement to feel good but a bit uncertain too. Love bombing looks a lot like a romantic courtship—at least at first sight.

Both involve extravagant displays of affection, an ever-increasing expression of feelings, a need to be together. In love bombing, the attention and emotions have an expiry date—they usually end or decrease when the other is already emotionally invested, and there is no more need to reel them in.

They Will Capitalise on Your Empathy

During the love-bombing phase, they make you feel special. You understand them more than anyone else, you are better than their exes, you are prettier, more attractive and you generally have better qualities than anyone else they have ever met. They are very good at identifying your weak spots and self-esteem issues.

But going further than that, they will capitalise on your empathy, and they won't hold back sharing vulnerable details of their lives with you. They are prone to ask for favours—emotional or otherwise, and they will make you feel that you are the only one who can save them.

If an empathetic individual is met with requests that involve them being the only one to help, they will do anything to live up to the expectations. They will free up their time, cancel plans with others, go out of their way to be there for their loved one.

Narcissists use this attitude to get what they want—an emotionally invested, enamoured individual, who is easy to manipulate.

The Mask Only Slips When You Are Invested Enough

The mask *will* slip, without exception. *But the timing is usually perfect.* It only happens after you're invested emotionally enough, when you are way deep in love, when you are more prone to look away seeing a red flag.

There are some subtle glimpses of their real character earlier on, but these signs are so rare and so ambivalent that it's easy to chalk them up to a bad day or an unfortunate coincidence.

Yet these signs will only reveal the narcissist's true self when it is already too difficult to walk away. The backhanded compliments turn into insults, and the jokes become so distasteful and questionable verbal abuse starts. They start to put you down— making your head spin, for it is usually so unexpected and unprecedented that you don't even have an answer to them.

They start acting differently and leave you wondering whether you have done anything wrong.

They apologise, but it's weightless, and it never changes their real behaviour. It simply serves to cover up their wrongdoings.

Abuse Evolves Gradually

Abuse doesn't start on day one, but it evolves gradually—as if they were trying to size you up, pushing your boundaries, testing how far they can go. They isolate you, slowly. First, just by asking for your time. Then by convincing you to choose them instead of anyone else around you. Then they remove themselves from situations where they should behave.

Soon, they'll manipulate you into not meeting anyone else by guilt-tripping you or causing major drama. Eventually, they may even forbid you from doing anything they don't like.

Verbal abuse starts with backhanded compliments and jokes, then they turn into covert, ambivalent put-downs, until it becomes downright abusive, belittling you, intimidating you or gaslighting you.

They stonewall you to punish you for any behaviour they dislike, and they become distant to exert power; they lie and manipulate to show you who is calling the shots. Then they come back apologising for hurting you, then do it all over again, *because they can.*

Ignoring the Signs

In a lot of abusive relationships, hindsight is 20/20 and looking back, it is easy to see how and when things went wrong. But when you are deep in it, everything happens according to a masterplan. You don't feel the need to escape until it's too late to run.

Realising the first signs, we tend to look for excuses and explanations to ease our cognitive dissonance, as it is difficult to accept that the one who is supposed to love us would deliberately hurt us. It's hard to make peace with the fact that our soulmate wants to manipulate us, instead of having our best interest in mind.

Regardless, it's essential to look for the signs. It's crucial that we trust our instincts and call our significant other out on their behaviour if something feels off.

But what is even more important is to know that abuse is *never* justified. Just because you trust someone, they shouldn't abuse your trust and kindness. Just because you crave love and intimacy, no one is entitled to manipulate you. Just because they used you for their own selfish purpose, it doesn't invalidate your feelings. Just because they are abusive, it doesn't mean you asked for it, or you deserved it.

Why Are We Addicted to (Bad) Love?

When someone is in an abusive relationship, they usually know it. They are aware that this is not how it should be, that something or everything is wrong, yet they are incapable of letting it go. **They feel addicted, but they can't put the finger on the "why".**

They do everything to please their abuser, to keep the relationship going, they even go to extreme lengths to defend them and downplay the seriousness of the maltreatment. They are lowering their standards and allowing things that they know they would have never allowed, and they do it over and over again, finding excuses, finding explanations, finding reason where there is none. They leave, and then they come back to the source of their terror. They believe that if they become more and better, then it will be different. They are willing to undergo considerable changes in looks, personality and lifestyle just to meet the moving goalpost of their abuser.

It is incomprehensible at best. Nonsensical and crazy at worst. It defies logic. It ignores reality. It goes against the pure survival instinct that we have.

In reality, there is an explanation.

Trauma bonding

Trauma bonding refers to the case when victims are forming a bond with someone who is clearly destructive to them. It has a huge effect on the victim, and while everything screams and shouts against it, *the bond is tough to break.*

Trauma bonding is the Stockholm Syndrome of a romantic relationship.

Stockholm syndrome as an idea was first coined by a Swedish psychiatrist and criminologist, Nils Bejerot. Bejerot was advising the Swedish police after a bank robbery in Stockholm, Sweden in 1973, that turned into a severe hostage situation. Four employees (three women and a man) of the bank were taken captive and held hostage when an attempted bank robbery failed. After being held captive for six days, the hostages, after their release, denied testifying against their captors, they defended them and even started to raise money for their defence. The term Stockholm Syndrome got to be used later on outside of Sweden, to aid the resolution of hostage situations.

Stockholm Syndrome is a condition, which causes the victim to develop a bond with their abuser—initially as a survival strategy.

The abuser is both the source of terror and comfort for the victim and no matter how irrational the attachment is, and several reasons keep the bond intact for a long time.

Trauma bonding becomes even stronger, when it comes to gradually increasing abusive events and alternating hopeful moments of loving periods. The intermittent reinforcement and hope make the victims feel drawn to those who hurt them. It seems irrational, but it is true.

> "In threatening and survival situations
> we look for evidence of hope — a small sign
> that the situation may improve."[6]

Love is Like Cocaine

On top of the crazy dynamics of the abuse cycle, intermittent reinforcement and trauma bonding is also linked to a biochemical addiction in our brains. A rational reason that explains why the cyclical nature of the abuse, the push and pull phenomenon strengthens the bond in case of abuse. A potent mix of chemicals, such as oxytocin, serotonin, dopamine, cortisol, and adrenaline are present in case of lust and attraction. From the first ecstasy to the last bit of withdrawal symptoms. It is causing real addiction, to make us want to come back for more, always more. One of these ingredients, dopamine is especially known for causing trauma bonding, as it is even more activated if there are intermittent dosage and deprivation. Being imposed to danger, and the lingering sensation of being at risk elevates the hormonal levels to a point, *where the feelings caused by the other can only be compared to drug use.*

In an exhaustive piece[7], Helen Fisher, the American anthropologist, human behaviour researcher, and self-help author, explains how the brain acts when in love.

According to Fisher, romantic love is an addiction. It is a positive addiction when the love is reciprocated, nontoxic, and appropriate; and a terribly negative addiction when one's feelings of romantic love are inappropriate, poisonous, unreciprocated, or formally rejected.

In one study she cites, when brains of happily-in-love participants and euphoric addicts (who just injected cocaine or opioids) are compared it is visible that many of the same regions in the brain became active. Another study showed that the region linked with addictions—like craving for heroin, cocaine, nicotine, alcohol, gambling, sex and food—fire up when feeling in love. Meaning, being happily in love means to be addicted to the partner—suggesting that romantic love is a natural addiction experienced by almost all human beings.

It starts with assigning a special meaning to the other—we start to focus on our partner intently. We can see an old friend with fresh eyes or a complete stranger suddenly occupying our thoughts. The occurrence of thoughts is random at first then it develops a pattern of intrusive thinking, when thoughts of the object of our love start to invade our mind.

We catch ourselves remembering how they smile, what they said, how they acted—and we immerse ourselves in the thought of them. Everything that happens to us somehow ends up triggering a thought of them: what would they think of this book, how would they solve their problems. Regardless of the time spent together, the minutes and hours together start to gain weight and we cherish them as memories, thinking regularly back on them.

Then these intrusive thoughts become more prevalent—according to studies they might occupy 85 to 100 percent of our days and nights—distracting us from everything else. During this time, we begin to focus on their traits—zooming in on aspects that are trivial. This is called **crystallisation,** when we see and understand their flaws, but we choose not to deal with them at all. We focus on the positive and musing about them we fall deeper and deeper.

Falling in love also involves craving, hope and uncertainty. In case of any positive response, we are over the moon. Any case of uncertainty can send us into a negative spiral and depression. These uncertain moments, eventually resolving, enhance the feeling of love—causing a phenomenon called **frustration attraction.**

There is a huge element of helplessness and irrational fears. Most lovers admit that their obsession is irrational and involuntary—supporting the theory that love is a biological, instinct-like addictive action, defying logic and escaping control.

Love is a roller coaster—and we jump on it, dreading the lows and living for the highs. It's beautiful and terrifying. Uncontrollable and irrational—but it's love.

It's all fun and games until someone ends the relationship.

Like any other addiction, romantic love can ruin us—especially if the object of love is taken away. fMRI scans show that brain regions responsible for deep attachment, physical pain and anxiety were active in test subjects—after having been rejected by their lovers.

Helen Fisher goes on saying: "activity in several of these brain regions has been correlated with the craving of cocaine addicts and other drugs. In short, as our brain scanning data show, these discarded lovers are still madly in love with and deeply attached to their rejecting partner. They are in physical and mental pain. Like a mouse on a treadmill, they are obsessively ruminating on what they've lost. And they are craving reunion with their rejecting beloved—addiction."

We all suffer from loss of love in our lives—only a few of us are lucky enough not to. When we get rejected, our first attempts are to get back the love that we lost—no matter the price. Then despair sets in, we give up hope and slip into depression. All these are linked to our brain's dopamine system. When we encounter any barriers to our feelings, the passion intensifies. Being dumped means that we just love more who rejected us, this is the frustration attraction. Adversity enhances love. When the reward is delayed, the dopamine system is still on—keeping love alive even more so. *We are addicted.*

In case of narcissistic abuse, the repetitive discard phases strengthen our feelings of love—and the intermittent reinforcement works in the abuser's favour. When we crave our lover who rejected us, it is easy to get dragged back again—it is like with an addiction, we just want one last fix, and then we swear to get off it.

Love is an addiction—just as real as any other addictive substances, in behavioural patterns and brain activity. Even when romantic love is not harmful, it is still characterised by intense craving and anxiety.

Being addicted to a loved one is not an individual character flaw—it's human nature. And if the love you are addicted to is bad, neurochemically your feelings make perfect sense.

Educating yourself about it and treating it as an addiction can help you in moving forward. If you know that your attraction is caused by biochemicals in your brain, it makes it easier to accept that you need to stay away—you need to go cold turkey and get the necessary distance.

Knowing that your feelings make you irrational in your choices can be a great motivation to decide despite your feelings and try to find ways to counteract your instinctive reactions.

It also suggests that you will have withdrawal symptoms and you need to fight through it. Getting one last fix will only throw you back into their arms—hindering the healing.

125

Is Mental Illness an Excuse for Abuse?

*"Until we have seen someone's
darkness, we don't really know who they are.
Until we have forgiven someone's darkness,
we don't really know what love is."* —
MARIANNE WILLIAMSON

When I met my ex, I felt I won the lottery. He was the most charming man I have ever met. He was funny and caring, he listened to me with such attention I never believed was possible and he told me all about himself. It wasn't too-good-to-be-true, because he was very honest about his shortcomings. He told me about his childhood, his traumas, his fears and hopes. He told me quite early on that he was suffering from a Cluster B personality disorder.

I wouldn't have figured that he had a mental illness, but I knew enough about people struggling with depression, panic attacks, PTSD to understand that mental illness can be unnoticeable from the outside in many cases. I never questioned it—I've always known better than that.

When he told me, I wasn't even alerted. I consider mental illness as a condition that can be part of our lives. You can live with it, you can function with it, you can tame it and control it. Knowing about it and admitting it is a huge thing—it takes a lot of courage, it means you open up and you show your most vulnerable side, you reveal a secret. I didn't ask anything more, as I said, it was quite early on, we were just getting to know each other.

I would have wanted to ask what it means for him, how he lives with it, does he take any medications, does he go to therapy, does he participate in self-help of any kind? But I didn't think it was appropriate. He admitted it and then became distant about it—that I respected and treated him with the utmost care and tact. I looked at him like he was some kind of wounded animal, desperately needing love and attention. His raw vulnerability made him very human, loveable and approachable. I loved him even more for it.

I googled it as soon as I got home and searched for all the symptoms, signs, treatments. It wasn't easy.

He told me Cluster B and nothing more. Checking out Cluster B personality disorders, none of them looked like him. None of them fitted the image of the guy I fell in love with.

I shrugged it away. After all, he told me that it is all under control. That he had come a long way and years of behavioural therapy and medication helped him overcome the worst of it, and now it is all under control.

I believed him. He was smart and funny and handsome, and he was as much in love with me as I was in love with him. I was telling myself that love means to love someone despite all his flaws and problems. It means to stand by the other, helping and supporting them when in need. And this is exactly what I was planning to do—to be there for him, in his darkest hours.

When things started to deteriorate and I started to see more of him, I understood why he was given the diagnosis of Cluster B. He was a mix of the different disorders' character traits. 'Borderline' and 'Narcissistic' with a bit of a 'Histrionic.' Later I could add the 'Antisocial' to the equation when I learned about him shoplifting, his prison time, his pub fights, and tire slashing stunts. Only it was way too late.

After we started to talk about it, he began to boast about being narcissistic. He also added psychopathy—and he was proud of it. Finally, he could make sense of his own coldness, callousness, ignorance and complete lack of empathy. There was a reason for all that—and he was happy about it!

The paradise he was taking me to soon turned into purgatory and hell. That's when he started to use his mental health condition as a shield and excuse.

Don't anger me today, this is one of those days...

He said that his chemical imbalance causes him to have bad days. I looked it up and found that Borderline personality disorder does have a certain chemical cycle, like an ebb and flow, and I even started to notice a pattern. I was planning our days around it, organising travel for good days only. Trying to stay away on bad days. It was a good plan, except it didn't work. It was at first a two-week cycle... then to my horror, it started to get shorter, to the point when it was a daily alternation of good days and bad days.

I am not questioning the chemical imbalance. But the cycle wasn't because of it. I only learned it later that he was following the exact pattern as every single abusive person. Honeymoon, tension, abuse...

You should have known better... you knew I would cheat on you, it's my disorder...

'Cluster B Histrionic' disorder is known for shallow emotion. Borderline behaviour, being reckless and irresponsible, unprotected and promiscuous, and sexually narcissistic is about the excessive need for attention. He said cheating on me was not a choice... it was coming from his disorder. But he also said he hated it and *he only loved me.*

I suggested a non-monogamous relationship, I didn't like to get jealous about random women who never meant anything for him. I told him it was okay with me.

He stopped the behaviour—I took away its power over me. He didn't need it because his brain was pushing him, he did it to hurt me and manipulate me. When I said it didn't bother me, he stopped it.

Don't leave me, I am troubled and broken...

Whenever I wanted to set boundaries, draw lines or when I called out on his behaviour, he went into defence mode. He not only played his part; he really was troubled and broken. When I gave an ultimatum, he was in tears, he promised everything, he said he would go to therapy, take his medication. Chemical imbalance, you know.

He never went to therapy more than once in a row. He stopped taking his anti-psychotic meds when his libido plummeted. He started to take testosterone against doctors' orders, to get his stamina and erection back. Too bad that testosterone is also responsible for aggression. And it just got worse.

Help me love myself more

At some point, his mental health issues were blamed on his parents, including that his dad never loved him. That his mom was too busy with his dad. He never got the attention he needed. He never learned how to love himself. And there I was, heartbroken to see my love in such a state. Of course, he is rude, of course, he is broken—no one taught him how to love properly. I will show him; me of all people. Talk about being naive.

I loved him more than anyone. But it was never enough. Nothing I said or did was enough. He always found some putdown, some insult, instilled doubt.

You need to save me, no one else can

He looked at me like a wounded animal. Clung to me like I was his lifeline. He wanted me by his side all the time. He didn't like me to see my friends, especially guys. He alienated me from my family. *He needed me*. Whenever I had something else to do, he pulled the disorder card, requested me to stay home, or do whatever he needed me to do. To save him was nothing major, it was about the little things. Think about sorting folders and photos at 1 am because that was going to calm him.

He used me. *I was his puppet*. I was to do exactly as he told me. He had power over me whenever he wanted. He knew I would do anything to avoid a midnight meltdown, so he made me stay up, to do his job, while he went to sleep.

I had to save him from his evil friends—telling him how talented he is and how they don't deserve him. Save him from his family who abandoned him— so it was just us against the world. Only to learn later that his family didn't abandon him at all. I had to save him from himself—*to walk on eggshells*, to pamper him, to admire him—to pull him out from his bad days. It was in my interest—very much so.

Mental health is a serious issue, I have never taken it lightly.

I know a lot of people who are struggling with it, fighting invisible battles day after day. And they are trying to fit in, to cope with it, to live a life where they are not causing harm to others—whenever they can avoid it. I know, because I have been there. And I knew it too well that pushing my own suffering onto others would not help me—so I avoided it whenever I could.

And I know quite a few jerks too, who were just simply rude, offensive, insensitive and toxic to others. They were causing harm because they can, they hurt because they chose to. He said hurtful things because he could. He was abusive because I allowed him to—by staying—and because he loved the thrill of the power, he had over me.

Maybe it was because of his condition that he was abusive. Maybe his demons were chasing him and telling him all those things that came later on out his mouth to hurt me. Maybe it was a chemical imbalance that made him hit me.

But regardless of his condition, he was abusive and aggressive.

And no matter what the reasons were behind it, *abuse was not justifiable*, it was not right—and it was always a choice. Mental illness if not curable is still treatable, manageable, controllable. Refusing therapy and medication is a choice—just like raising a hand was one. Not giving up on alcohol was his call—and I paid the price for it

Abuse is abuse—no matter where you look at it from. It had to stop. Sadly, usually leaving was the only solution.

Maybe he did suffer from his disorder but the rest of the world, and primarily I, suffered from it more—because of him.

4. LIFE WITH THE NARCISSIST

The Flawed Dynamics of a Narcissistic Relationship

Every relationship type has certain dynamics to it—and they evolve with the relationship. Some evolve organically, some need external help and a lot of self-reflection. There are ups and downs, there are phases, there are periods that are better than others. A genuine relationship is built on intimacy, commitment, trust, consistency, progression, shared values, love and care. It is built on a promise that the partners watch out for each other, support each other and they do it in a predictable and reliable way.

It's only natural to grow apart or grow closer, to develop shared interests or part ways if the level of compatibility is not sufficient enough to maintain the relationship. But when it comes to a relationship with someone with a narcissistic personality disorder, the patterns are predictable—but not in a good way. The biggest problem is that when we enter such a relationship, we have no idea what it will evolve into.

We are not meant to be alone and self-sufficient. Us, human beings are wired to be in company, genetically coded to be accepted and appreciated by others. Back in the days, our survival depended on it. Only those who were part of the tribe—then later the community and society,—survived. Isolation is an evolutionary dead-end; it has been used as torture for prisoners; social isolation these days is a root cause for mental health issues and destructive maladaptive behaviours.

Being with others, appreciated and validated by our peers is our only way to a happy and fulfilled life. If we want to experience intimacy, loving ourselves is simply not enough. We need to learn how to love ourselves, how to appreciate ourselves—and we learn it from the people around us.

In our individualistic society, we are expected to be self-made, self-sufficient, capable to solve everything on our own. We should avoid being dependent on external validation, our strength and self-love is supposed to come from the inside.

But self-love is not a conscious decision; it roots from our core personality and conditioning. It depends on how early we learn our self-worth and how quickly we can build or rebuild our capacities to love ourselves. Those who are successful are never lone warriors—they all have a solid emotional background, that is worth a lot more than self-talk. We need external validation—to be able to accept ourselves.

We long to be loved and cherished. We long for love and intimacy. The narcissist is giving us just exactly what we need—in the beginning.

When I met my partner, who later on turned out to be a narcissist, I thought I met the love of my life, my soul mate, the one I have been waiting for all my life. We matched on a dating app and in no time, we were chatting, he was charming and funny; he knew the right answers to *everything*. It was obvious that he's not slow. He used finely crafted pickup lines, spiced with morsels of information he had taken from my profile and from what he learnt from our short conversation. He was paying attention. Big time. And I was bathing in it.

It was refreshing to chat with someone who controlled the situation, who knew what he wanted. He was straightforward and subtle at once. An expert. I should have taken it as a red flag, but this was a dating app—there is no shame in wordplay.

He was quick to fix a date, he complimented me all the time and made me feel special. We matched on

Monday and met on Wednesday afternoon, for a coffee, because he wanted to get to know me better. We spent long hours talking and walking, and he was just as charming and fun to be with as it appeared from the conversations that we had. It was going well.

Things escalated quickly. He promised he would call, and he did. We agreed to meet again, and we did. He showered me with his attention, bombarded me with text messages, we stole moments of our workdays just to spend minutes together.

It was all great and I was falling fast. He told me the same, he confessed he loved me on our second date, I was holding back so it took me a month to tell him I loved him. I wanted to savour it, taking it slow, but he was jumping in it, with full force and such enthusiasm that left no room for taking it slow. We were *"meant to be together"*. We had fireworks, great sex, we were falling in love, he was becoming a part of my life in no time.

At the time I had no idea that I met a narcissist, and him "falling in love" was his normal modus operandi. He reeled me in, he made me believe that I was special, that he has never felt this way. He told me and gave me everything I have ever wanted in a relationship. He was always around, always there, always texting, always talking and listening, always paying attention, always touching me and holding me close. He *never* stopped showering me with his love, affection and attention.

I thought it was love. But it was not love. It was love bombing. This is how the cycle starts. And it is followed by devaluation and then finally by discard. The phases between idealisation and devaluation can repeat endlessly—before discarding. Eventually discard will happen too—which can be as short and as long as they want it.

Discard can be final—they disappear forever, or they can hoover you back—throwing you back to square one, when the idealisation phase will begin again.

Let's see how the cycle looks like before we deep-dive into the phases.

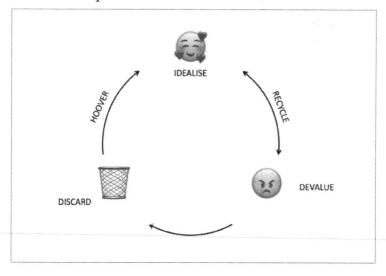

The Narcissistic Dynamics: Idealisation, Devaluation, Discard

Idealisation or Love Bombing

The first people to use the term "love bombing" weren't psychiatrists and it wasn't used in relation to romantic relationships: they were members of the Unification Church of the United States. In the 1970s, their founder and leader Sun Myung Moon said:

"Unification Church members are smiling all of the time, even at four in the morning. The man who is full of love must live that way. When you go out witnessing, you can caress the wall and say that it can expect you to witness well and be smiling when you return. What face could better represent love than a smiling face? This is why we talk about love bomb; Moonies have that kind of happy problem."

The cult leaders Jim Jones, Charles Manson, and David Koresh weaponised love bombing, using it to con followers into committing mass suicide and murder. Pimps and gang leaders use love bombing to encourage loyalty and obedience as well.

Love bombing is an attempt to influence another person with over-the-top displays of attention and affection. It's not just about romantic gestures, but it includes lots of romantic conversation, long talks about "our future," and long periods of staring into each other's eyes.

It works this well because us humans have a natural need to feel good about who we are, and often we can't fill this need on our own. Sometimes the reason is situational, brought on by an event, like divorce or job loss. Other times, it's more constant and traces back to our childhood. Whatever the source, love bombers are experts at detecting low self-esteem and exploiting it.

Love bombing differs from romantic courtship, but not at first sight. The difference becomes visible after two people are officially a couple. If these extravagant displays of affection continue indefinitely, if actions match words, and there is no devaluation phase, then it's probably not love bombing. But if it is love bombing, then brace yourself for impact, as it will just get worse.

Narcissists are the perfect charmers. They know all the right words to say and they will gain your trust quickly. They share overly personal, gut-wrenching stories from their past. They will be obsessed with you, talk about the future with high hopes for you two. They will tell you they've never felt this way before. They will flatter you, overly so, in such a fashion that they make you feel like they're running out of time and each second must be spent with you. Their smile radiates warmth and their eyes twinkle at the sight of you. And just when you can't seem to help but also smile from ear to ear and waiting to hear from them, you realize you're hooked.

Devaluation

After the Idealisation phase, there is an abrupt shift in the type of attention, from affectionate and loving to controlling and angry, making unreasonable demands.

Once they feel confident that they've secured you, the mask slips and they begin to show their true colours. The narcissist's admiration can end as quickly and abruptly as it began. It's harsh, unexpected and heartbreaking. They become cold, inattentive and indifferent. They become bored easily, and the emotional void you helped them fill at the initial stage begins to wear off. They are now wondering if you can give them what they need; if you're worthy; if you're special. Certainly, you cannot be since they no longer feel the high, they initially felt.

They disappear and dismiss your feelings and *you are left wondering what went wrong*. The devalue phase is a crucial part of the cycle, they deliberately mess with your head. This is classic psychological conditioning: the idealisation is the positive reinforcement (you do what I want, and I'll shower you with love), the devaluation is the negative consequence (you did something wrong, so I'm punishing you).

If you point out any of their wrongdoings, you'll be met with resistance and criticism. A narcissist will not take any blame. They will begin to undermine you, while putting themselves on a pedestal, speaking highly of themselves. Their self-worth is completely dependent on your and others' admiration. Once you take that away from them, once you abandon them, they no longer have need for you.

During the devaluation phase they use manipulative abuse tactics spiced up with instances of love-bombing to create enough confusion.

They will give you the silent treatment—leaving you for days, even disappearing in the middle of the night, not returning your calls and texts, leaving you confused, hurt and worried. Then they come back and pretend nothing happened. If you point out their unfair treatment, they will call you clingy, overly sensitive and compare you to all the others who couldn't respect their need for space.

They will stonewall you, refusing to talk to you and answer your questions. Or they will get into circular nonsensical conversations. They will belittle you and ridicule you with overt or covert putdowns. They will give you ultimatums that you can't possibly win.

The point is to get you to beg and plead, to apologise and shower them with your admiration again. Also, they want to prove their superiority and exert power. The emotional manipulation is a power play, to show you who's in charge.

Discard

Then there comes a point when you are no longer of any value to the narcissist. They will easily humiliate you, leave you for another, compare you to their exes and future targets. They ignore you and ghost you without looking back. This is intended to hurt and traumatise you without any closure.

Rejection always hurts—every time. We can't be old enough or experienced enough, emotional rejection hurts just as much as physical pain. Rejection hurts—no matter if it's romantic rejection, sexual, if it happens in a friendship or within family or at work. Romantic rejection hurts because romantic love activates a dopamine loop that is now broken.

For our brain, rejection feels the same as feeling physical pain. fMRI studies show that the same areas of the brain fire up when we experience rejection and physical pain, and the brain has no way of telling whether it was physical hurt or emotional one. Both hurt—a lot.

We have a fundamental need to belong to a group, to people, to a significant other. When we get rejected, this need becomes destabilized and our emotional pain is enhanced by this emotional uncertainty. To counterbalance this unstable situation, it is suggested to reconnect with those who love us or reaching out to members of groups to which we feel strong affinity and who value and accept us.

Rejection creates surges of anger and aggression. Studies show that rejection was a greater risk for adolescent violence than drugs, poverty, or gang membership. Even mild rejections can lead people to take out their aggression on innocent bystanders. Violence against women is another example of the strong link between rejection and aggression—taken to an extreme level. Especially when rejection happens in a sexual situation, the rejected party might lose their temper, not taking no for an answer, regardless whether the rejection was addressed to him personally, or caused by a situation. Rejection feels terrible and people tend to hurt the closest to them.

However, much of that aggression coming from rejection is also turned inward and makes us question ourselves. A possible response to romantic rejections is looking for and finding fault in ourselves. We tend to ignore the circumstances and the fact that most romantic rejections are a matter of poor fit and a lack of chemistry, incompatible lifestyles, wanting different things at different times. Blaming ourselves deepens the emotional pain we feel and makes it harder for us to recover emotionally.

Rejection does not respond to reason. Participants were put through an experiment[8] in which they were rejected by strangers. The experiment was rigged—the "strangers" were confederates of the researchers. Surprisingly, though, even being told that the "strangers" who had "rejected" them did not actually reject them did little to ease the emotional pain participants felt.

Hoovering

In this relationship everything happens on their terms. They can choose to discard you at any point, but they can also decide that they still need you for some kind of validation—affection, sex, money or revenge.

If you already see through them and you want to leave, they won't let you. You feel that you can never leave. They are entitled to play with you, leave you and when they get bored with someone else, they reserve their rights to come back at any time. At least this is what their mentality demonstrates.

And they do come back, they always do. And the vicious cycle begins. They act like the same charming person that first lured you in, perhaps throwing in some more lucrative and attractive promises, such as more affection. This is a tactic to again gain your trust, make you believe they're remorseful, that they can and will change, only to use you once again. They revel in the fact that you were so devastated, hurt and confused. It gives them a sense of power, and there is nothing to stop them—as you are playing along with them, you are a sensitive human being, acting the role out perfectly as they planned it out for you.

This phase is called Hoovering, when they suck you back into the relationship, they throw you back to the love bombing phase, showering you with their love, promising that they will change and never ever leave you. They show remorse, they apologise, and they do everything they can to assure that you are hooked again—providing them with what they need, their supply.

When we are in love and our lover just rejected us, we want nothing more but to get back together with them. We are trying to find ways to talk to them, to reason with them, to make them see that they made a mistake. We want them to miss us and we want them to come back and show us how much they love us.

Among the abuse survivors there is a typical question: *Where is my hoover?* When will they come back? While these questions are valid, they are coming from the wrong place. It takes a lot of strength to break the addiction, and being hoovered doesn't help in moving forward, growing or healing. It throws us back to the middle of it—the whole chaos starts again, we sit back on the roller coaster, and what's even worse, we do it willingly.

Narcissists know this. They know they have power over us, and they use this power to suck out as much fuel as they possibly can. They also tend to have a sixth sense—as if they would know exactly when we are about to move on, just to come back and give us a nudge, pushing us back into the hole we just got out of.

There is no timeline for hoovering—some come back within weeks. Some wait months to give a sign. Some report that their partner left them and came back trying to seduce them after years of being completely off the radar.

Hoovering is about narcissistic supply, the energy that they crave, that they need to survive with their own empty souls. If they run out of suppliers, they will try to get it from people who were good at providing for them. They will try to get back to the relationship, or if it's impossible because you resist, they will do anything in their power to extract other types of energy—negative energy is just as good. This is when the smear campaigns and vindictive actions happen.

Narcissistic Supply, Injury and Rage

Human beings need appreciation and feedback from people around them. We need to be loved and cherished, we need approval and admiration. If possible, we avoid criticism. The cues from the external world shape us and reinforce our behavioural patterns.

It's only normal—and the narcissists do the same. But there are huge differences in normative needs and narcissistic needs, both in quantity and quality.

The narcissist is an addict of *external validation*. They are the mental equivalent of a sex addict, and alcoholic or a gambler. Their needs are insatiable. The void in them and their lack of established self require them to seek external reinforcement to be able to function. Their whole behaviour revolves around getting extreme quantities of attention—while any negative feedback is crushing them. The positive feedback is strengthening their False Self—a constructed, biased image of superiority and vanity. This False Self is what they believe to be real.

The False Self serves to maintain this fictitious version of themselves, one of an omnipotent, invincible, charming, interesting, intelligent and rich person—regardless of reality.

The feedback can come from anywhere, from family members, colleagues, neighbours, children and intimate partners. They will go to extreme lengths to assure a constant flux of admiration and reassurance of their False Self. They will do everything to make people believe the image they project; they will ask for or extort the affirmation or applause.

For they are incapable of maintaining their self without the external admiration, they rely on what comes at them from the outside. The energy that keeps them going is the praise and recognition coming from others. This is their supply—the narcissistic supply.

The Narcissistic Supply

By definition, the narcissistic supply is a psychological concept which describes a type of admiration, interpersonal support or sustenance drawn by an individual from their environment. The term is typically used in a negative sense, describing a pathological or excessive need for attention or admiration that does not take into account the feelings, opinions or preferences of other people.

It is any form of attention that confirms their existence, assures their sense of superiority, uniqueness and entitlement. Positive sources can be:

- compliments,
- gestures,
- love and caring,
- admiration,
- approval,
- affirmation,
- respect,
- applause,
- celebrity status,
- money,
- sexual conquest.

Energy can also come from negative emotions, for even disdain means that they get the necessary display of attention. Negative sources can be:

- rage,
- being hurt,

- disappointment,
- fear or being feared,
- jealousy,
- confusion,
- threats.

There are different categories of suppliers for the narcissist.

Primary Narcissistic Supply

The Primary Supply for the Narcissist is the person they are spending the most time with, whose attention and affection they draw from on a daily basis. It is usually a partner within an intimate relationship—who provides them with their basic needs regularly. They rely on this source more than on anything else, which also means that the Primary Supply is getting the biggest share of the abuse.

Secondary Narcissistic Supply

As nothing is enough, the Primary Supply cannot do the job fully for the narcissist. The narcissist is in constant need of finding new sources—to ensure never to run out of the fuel that the energy provides.

This is why they have a whole array of admirers, friends and attentive co-workers. They work hard on getting positive feedback from as many people as they can. The secondary supplies are not integral parts of their lives, but if the energy starts to become inevitably lower from a primary supply, it is possible that they promote a secondary one to become primary.

As long as the flux of energy is intact, they don't care about where it comes from.

Narcissistic Injury or Rage

Imagine a two-year old having a meltdown for not getting what they want. For a toddler it could be about anything—their toys being too far, the morning cereal is the wrong colour, or simply the time has come to put some socks on. When dealing with toddlers, parents are used to drama-over-nothing situations. They can't yet regulate their emotions, they don't recognise priorities, they are learning and testing their own boundaries.

Narcissists, in a sense, are grown up tantrum-throwing toddlers.

If they don't get their expected dose of attention, affection and admiration—or even worse, they face criticism, disrespect of ignorance—they can spiral into a meltdown quicker than a toddler. Their False Self is built of the blocks of external validation, and if it's taken away or the dose is not right, their whole ego starts crumbling down.

They are terrified of negative feedback—*because it takes away their sense of superiority.*

If they are given feedback at work, if something they are doing flops, if they face sexual rejection—which should be normal in any relationship—they take it as if their whole existence was questioned.

They suffer narcissistic injury and enter the raging narcissist.

All the narcissistic abuse comes from their perceived injuries. In their minds, everything should revolve around them. No one else is important enough, nothing is urgent enough—until their needs are met. And it's impossible, because they are continuously raising their expectations. They can suffer injury from an uninterested glance, a half-hearted cheer, a sentence that they misunderstand, something that disrupts their plans or someone cancelling on them, regardless of the reason.

They blow everything out of proportion, and they are quick to shift the blame. This is how co-workers become idiots. This is how a closed shop becomes the enemy of the state. This is how a slow internet connection can ruin their days and send them into a drinking spree. They are impulsive and impatient—they can't wait and won't wait.

Their partners are in the front line of these suffered injuries. They are the buffer to soften the blow. They are the ones taking the blame for not knowing that the shop would be closed, the internet would drag, or the coffee would be too hot.

Anything that disturbs their perfect world—where they deserve everything immediately—is a source of narcissistic injury and it sends them into a narcissistic rage. Their efforts to manage the cognitive dissonance usually aimed at the innocent bystanders—colleagues, kids, partners—who won't understand how such a tiny thing can cause such turbulence.

The ultimate narcissistic injury occurs if someone neglects or abandons them. It can be a distant colleague who used to be laughing at their jokes but now they have other things to do—they will get on their blacklist immediately. It can be an ex-lover who refuses to play along with them any longer, for they finally started to live their lives. It can be their partner who finally has enough and decides to put a foot down and draw boundaries, wants to leave.

Why Do Narcissists Lie?

Lying is saying something or leaving out something important with the intent of creating a false impression. To a certain extent everybody lies—but the frequency and intensity of it and the motive behind it vary by person. Whether someone is lying out of fear, manipulation or pride— the fact remains, lying is destructive and can be harmful. Moreover, it can be addictive, for the web of lies create a false pattern that cannot be maintained only with further lies. The addictive nature of it makes it difficult to stop, but if you weigh the positives and negatives of it, you will see how it can ruin relationships, completely shatter trust and make you lose your integrity.

Children learn how to lie usually to avoid punishment—and if they get away with it, it might signal for them that lying is paying off. Adults lie—telling white lies, omitting parts of the truth—to protect their loved ones or for some other reason. We all have the capacity to tell lies—better or worse—and it is up to our personal values and integrity to draw a line between the truth and a lie.

Pathological lying is not a clinical diagnosis, but it can be a symptom of a personality disorder or a manic episode. The narcissist lies compulsively—and is so used to telling lies and creating their false self that it's difficult even for them to tell when they lied.

The number and nature of lies that I have come across when living with a narcissist always shocked me. Some of his lies were so blatantly obvious, that I was the one left feeling awful. Some lies were subtle, almost true, except for some little tingling feeling that was suggesting something was off.

The narcissist is stripped of empathy, remorse and guilt.

There is literally nothing to stop them from forming lies in their heads or actually saying them out loud. They lack the moral compass to guide them toward good and decent behaviour. Nothing is off-limits, especially when lying can serve their interests and if they think they can profit from omitting or altering the truth. In addition, the narcissist is thriving on drama, rejoicing when there is emotional chaos, and risking being caught is giving them even more motivation to craft a better, more artistically fabricated lie.

When I called out my narcissistic ex on lying, he laughed in my face and told me he did it, because he could. He said: *"You're no challenge to me. I could do it one hand tied behind my back."*

He didn't do it to cover up something, he didn't do it to make himself look better, he merely did it because he knew he could get away with it, and even if he didn't, he enjoyed how it made me suffer.

So Why Do Narcissists Lie?

To get an emotional reaction

Narcissistic people thrive on the energy of emotions, be them positive or negative. They lie to make you fall in love, to get you infatuated and obsessed, to make you adore and admire them. But also, they will lie to hurt you, get you frustrated, anxious or angry. Negative emotions have just as much energy as positive ones—if not more. As they are incapable of feeling many emotions, they feed off others that they are so good at manipulating to meet their needs. They have to tell lies because they need this energy, they need to fulfil their sense of entitlement, break through a boundary, escape a consequence. Lying is a necessary survival mechanism.

To exert control

The narcissistic person is empty inside, they have nothing but a void, they have no real traits to be attracted to. They lack the self-worth that would allow them not to be concerned about their environment. They need to control what happens around them, who does what, who reacts how to their presence or absence. Lies are ensuring them to stay in control, by making them seen better than they are, by altering the power dynamics and ensuring always the upper hand. Also, lies allow escaping responsibility—which would cause any other decent human being to refrain from positioning themselves falsely.

To escape consequences

The narcissist knows that there are consequences to his actions, but he chooses not to be bothered about them in general. They refuse culpability by telling lies—small ones and big ones. At work, in a relationship, in bed, at the altar, at court. As I said, nothing is off-limits when it comes to shaking off responsibility.

They lie out of habit

The positive outcome from lying is so significant compared to any negative consequence, that they are compelled to lie frequently, so it becomes a habit. They get so used to lying that telling the truth becomes the uncomfortable rare event. Lying comes easily and they get such an expert at it, that it takes a very seasoned, unbiased and suspecting individual to spot it once it's told with utmost conviction.

The lie is better than the truth

If the truth is not meeting the needs of the narcissistic, then there is nothing else to do but to modify it. The truth is a lot less important than their entitlement, their need for being loved, admired, validated. At a certain point, they fail to see the world as it is, they only see it through their distorted perceptions—either letting go of reality completely or by choosing to see it in its fabrication.

It's all a game

Lying is all a game for the narcissist. They enjoy watching how the lie is bought and they enjoy telling further lies to a more impressive story. They praise themselves when their elaborate lies are not unravelled, yet even if they are, they don't care about the contradicting details as they don't face the consequences. This appeals to their high sense of entitlement and proves their high cognitive function. It makes them feel omnipotent, creator of the world. Constructing, defending and justifying their lies are a great achievement.

To create confusion

Lying is part of their gaslighting tactics, when they make you question your own perception of reality. *They enjoy creating confusion and they adore the drama all around.* What could better serve their purposes than a few hurt and confused people around them?

What Are Their Biggest Lies, And What Do They Really Mean By Them?

1. I would never lie to you.

They would and they do, and this is the biggest lie of all. The real advantage is to start the brainwashing early, to convince you about how honest and decent they are, a person of integrity. By the time the discrepancies are found out, this lie has already been believed—creating even more confusion, as the cruel actions and previously said convincing words are so far apart.

2. She was obsessed with me.

A common narcissist tactic is a triangulation, where at least one more person is involved in the relationship, at least verbally. This is usually an obsessed and unstable ex, meaning that the ex has probably discovered their infidelities and discrepancies, maybe even exposed them. The only way the narcissist can preserve their image is by discrediting those who discovered the face behind the mask. This means that the past victim might be out there confused and desperately looking for clues to make sense of it all. It is also a hint that after they are done with you, you will become this angry, desperate, obsessive victim—and that they will ridicule you with their current victim.

3. We have so much in common, it's unbelievable.

No, it's not, it's calculated. They studied you and copied you and they are using your own words and phrases to lure you in. Unbelievable match in likes and dislikes, favourite food, favourite music and places. It's like you were created to be soulmates. *They are mirroring you*—this is how you feel so familiar around them because they are copying your motions, gestures, facial expressions, words, everything. You see yourself in them because this is what they want you to do. They morph into someone you have always wanted until you are completely hooked. Then, and only then, they will let the mask slip—to reveal someone else, creating the utmost confusion.

4. I'm just checking in, love you.

They don't love you, but they are checking in to see if they still have control over you. To check if you miss them and want them. They will pop by and then disappear unannounced, to cause confusion and pain and make you suffer, only to come back with a huge smile and some atrocious excuse—that you will let go, being happy that they're back.

5. Cheating is morally wrong.

They get extremely bored in a long term committed relationship, so they will be out and about, collecting admiration and praise, trophies and probably Sexually Transmitted Infections too. They thrive on making people competing for them, they enjoy the chaos of love triangles. So, they cheat. Happily and unapologetically. However, cheating is wrong if *you* do it. You are not allowed to give your attention to anyone else, you are their toy to exploit, to play with, to lie to. The double standards are so obvious that it hurts to watch.

6. I changed.

They will open up about all their past wrongdoings and bad attitudes, being a player, being promiscuous, being a cheater—only to say that they changed. It is nothing more than a tactic to assure you that no one ever could save them from being a wreck, but here you are, you managed. You saved them, you lifted them up, you made them change. Who doesn't want to hear that? That they have such a great positive influence on another human being? They have absolutely no intention to change—yet saying this will benefit them in more ways than you would imagine. They put the responsibility on you, just like the fox says in The Little Prince, that you are responsible for what you have tamed. They inflate your sense of importance, to make you feel special and worthy—ensuring that they can play their games

165

for an even longer time without being caught or called out.

7. I am sorry.

This is the worst of all. Sorry as a word is a filler. It is weightless, absolutely lacking any meaning. It is said only because it is expected, not because they feel sorry. They have no remorse, no guilt, not afraid of consequences, never taking responsibility. *It's just words, no actions.* And sorry without acting upon it is just another manipulation tactic you should be careful about.

Sex with the Narcissist

The best sex I've ever had was both pure and dirty. It was about surrendering so wholly to the other that I could stop thinking about the world, I could just be myself—with him. It was connection at its best—spiced with immense love that made it even more special.

Sex has always been about connection for me. Even in casual dating, even during a one-night stand—it has always been about the connection between two human beings that made it fascinating. Or the lack of it made it boring or downright terrible.

In every healthy relationship, sex is a means of connecting with the other on an intimate level. It is allowing us to be vulnerable, opening up, trusting, experimenting, accepting flaws and learning about turn-ons and turn-offs. It is a fantastic journey—even better if there is love involved.

Sex with the narcissist is a unique, terrifying and devastating experience. It consists of both heaven and hell—with the boundaries blurring together so much that it's impossible to see the way out.

The only thing I know is that the sex was amazing. But how? How could he be so perfectly what I wanted him to be?

First of all, it's not just him personally.

Being the master of sex and a master manipulator when it comes to sex is quite common for narcissists. It's like they were cut out from the very same fabric, with slight differences only.

If you ever have the misfortune to get involved with a narcissist, it has to be said that when it comes to sex, they are amazing. Well, maybe amazing is not the proper word.

Imagine that you take a porn star who knows his way around their partner's body with eyes closed and one hand tied behind his back. Add the exquisite passion from an Italian lover—as you've seen in movies. And spice it with the spoken charms of a motivational speaker who seems to be in love with you—and your happiness and pleasure make his world go around.

To get really good at sex needs three things:

- being tuned in on the other,
- lots of practice
- and enthusiasm.

The narcissist has it all.

Sex is a power play for them, to get what they want—the energy from your love, your infatuation and even from your disappointment and anger.

Mind-Blowing Sex

Because of the personality disorder and its traits, sex for the narcissist is about power. It is about being in control, and it always has a hidden agenda. To get what they want—power, need for control, and desperate need for positive reinforcement,—nothing is sacred.

The blissful and exceptional experience starts as passionate, loving and caring, only to give way later on to forceful, manipulative, detached sexual encounters, abusive events, and non-consensual intercourse.

Sex with my narcissistic ex was mind-blowing and unbelievable. It was consistently satisfying, and it got better by the minute: ultimate pleasure, earth-moving orgasms, incredible chemistry and connection and love, love, love.

Following his carefully orchestrated tactics, the line between sex and love started to get blurred in my mind, and then it disappeared completely. Every sexual act was a sign of love. And anytime when it came to love, it had to be linked to sex. I was conditioned to this; I was taught this. Like a puppy, I learned, because the reward was great. And when the boundaries were pushed too far with the sex, I considered it as a sign of immense love.

So how did this heavenly experience turn into something abusive and harmful? There are quite a few common traits when it comes to sexuality with a narcissistic:

Easy Validation

Sex is the ultimate validation for the narcissist. Making love is a skill that he perfected throughout the years, taken to the point of mastery with all the women he had slept with before you. Not every lover of the narcissist makes it to become a fuel source like you, there is a whole array of trial-and-error lovers. With them, he is practicing sex with no intention to get anything else out of them.

Through all the women he practiced how to touch, how to please, how to pleasure. He has been using them to learn the clues, to understand the meaning of moans, he learnt how to take directions. He is like a sponge, he watches, observes and absorbs everything just to get better. Each act of sex is a validation for him. He is the perfect lover and rejoices in his own entitled self.

How can you be sure that he slept with a lot of women? He will tell you. If he is sex-obsessed enough, he will know the exact number, maybe with notes and remarks and learnings. This is his life. Of course, it matters to him.

Obsessing About His Performance

The narcissist cares about himself and himself only. Everything he does is for himself, *to fill the void he feels about his own life.* Sex is to prove his stamina, to confirm his skills, to prove that he is capable of giving pleasure—as it provides him feedback both about his performance and his control too.

The conversation about his size, his stamina started as sexy talk to spice up our sex life. Until it turned into a futile struggle from my side, trying to convince him that he is the best lover I have ever met. Soon it became a stress factor—when he started to question my compliments and started the name-calling. After all, how on earth could I have known that he is better than others unless I had sex with everyone. Which I must have done. Obviously. Jealousy became part of our lives, leading to arguments, fights, and beatings.

Mixing Sex And Love Deliberately

Love is sex. Sex is love.

A narcissistic individual is incapable of loving anyone else but himself. What he does is not love. Love has no value for him, but he is fully aware how much it means for any regular individual. Pretending love is the easiest way to get sex. He rarely admits that he wants sex only. He is willing to jump through the hoops of a committed relationship, because he knows that being emotionally invested will lead to easier access to sex—on his terms.

Nothing is off-limits, he is willing to promise everlasting love, he is willing to wait to lull your instincts. He mixes love into sex and he always mixes sex into love. Sex is his love language and he uses it to mesmerise you. He creates a confusing positive feedback loop of feeling loved and wanted—to harvest the admiration and the unconditional love from you, in the form of sex acts.

There was a point, where I would have done anything to please him, I was so addicted to everything he has done to me, that noticing the red flags was impossible as they were an integral part of the tapestry of our relationship. It was the thrill of things I have never tried. Now I know that I have never tried them for a good reason—being way out of my comfort zone.

They Know You

After a string of terrible or 'meh' dates, it is an amazing feeling to finally meet someone who is attentive. He wants to get to know you. He wants to know everything about you. He is curious about your childhood, your family, your fears and hopes. He wants to know you and show you how much he accepts you unconditionally—it's such a great feeling.

This is the period when he is getting to know you, when he is internalising your personality so that later he can mirror it back to you.

He always says the right things. You have these serendipity moments, when you realize that he is just exactly what you wanted. He wants to know everything so he can show you later how much alike you are.

It sounds a bit of an overkill, but this is an investment. You are going to give them what they want—your love, your energy, your admiration. For that, he is willing to fake that he is interested, he is willing to listen to all your sob-stories and hurt and enthusiasm. He is observing you; he is paying attention. *You think it's love — but it's grooming.*

Mirroring Your Personality

With a narcissist you will have the soulmate feeling all the time. You are meant to be. They always know the right answers. They always know what to do. They know how to make you smile. They know you enough to become exactly what you want them to be. The million aha-moments when you realize they love the same things, they adore the same positions, they shy away from the same. You fall for them because they are familiar. You trust them because you see yourself in them. You dare to open up, and you feel that your needs and desires are validated—on every level.

Sex And Pleasure On Their Terms Only

The initial attention and focus that was there to reel me in turned into seeking his pleasure only. He was throwing me breadcrumbs as intermittent reinforcement, so I shouldn't get frustrated enough to leave. He was balancing on edge-giving me the bare minimum to live on and raising the bar for me to please and satisfy him.

He knew how much I liked it, so he refused to give sex or tied it to conditions that I couldn't meet. He criticised my oral skills to get me to the point of hating it and being scared of it—only to decide that he will teach me how to do it properly. He took great pride in being able to pleasure me, at times, even when I was dead tired to have another orgasm—yet my body betrayed me and went along with his wish. It was a kind of torture, and yes, you can have too many orgasms—to the point of being terrified of it.

Sex-Breadcrumbing

They respect you and they are the champions of consent at first. You can say no—anytime. You are respected, your 'no' is respected. But they will take it a little too far. Had you said no to them, then they will stop having sex with you for days or even weeks. This is how much they respect you. They will even spell it out, that they won't reach out to you, for you expressed that you didn't want it and they understand. It is a lesson, it is to teach you never ever say no to them.

What you can't have you will want even more. It's psychological warfare, the ultimate intermittent reinforcement. If you need to wait or even somewhat beg for what you want, it will make you appreciate it even more—and he knows it.

He will throw you a couple of morsels and then wait until you beg for forgiveness. Then he gives you the best of the best, to show you what you missed when you said no. It is conditioning you to never disobey.

Withdrawal Of Sex As A Punishment And Porn Addiction

As part of their toolbox the withdrawal of sex—as the withdrawal of love—is quite prevalent. It is one of the manipulation techniques to take away what matters to you, what validates you. Without a warning or any particular reason, they can take their attention away, refuse to have sex, refuse to even sleep in the same bed with you.

Porn addiction for a narcissistic is a common thing; it's another item in the control-game. Watching the multitude of porn videos online, he has the power and the control only a click away. The internet provided lots of material to compensate for what you didn't do. And if they are unhappy by your performance, there are always other, younger, prettier girls that can get the job done. He insulted me in every way possible, criticising my skills, my body, my willingness. And he openly watched porn and masturbated in a way so I can see it. Explicitly saying that he has to do it alone, as I am incapable of giving him what he needs. I realized only later that the withdrawal was both to punish me and to be able to indulge in his addiction—while making me feel guilty about it.

Sex On The Borderline Of Consent

For the narcissistic, the first few months of love bombing is the conditioning period to condition the victim to agree to have sex whenever he wanted. Besides seeking his pleasure, it is deliberate, a power play again. Right on the borderline of consent—why would you say no, when previously you felt great about being desired to this extent?

He did as he pleased to do; he didn't care about my feelings or if I was ready. When I asked him to stop, he claimed it would be quick, and I can go back to sleep, but I turn him on so much he cannot go back to sleep. *It could be a compliment, right?* Except it wasn't. And when I finally agreed, he took his sweet time and kept asking why I didn't enjoy it. I didn't ask for it, sleep was my only desire, yet refusing him would have led to a terrible fight in the middle of the night. And I knew better.

The Pressure To Do Something Unwanted Or Risqué

By asking for something unusual or risqué, the narcissist is proving yet again his power over you. He is pushing you further and further out of your comfort zone-requesting it all for you to prove your love for him. His boundaries are very fluid; nothing is really off-limits—except when you comply with his wish, only to be condemned for doing as he wanted. After all, who would do this kind of thing anyway? Leaving you baffled and shocked—disarmed by a sentence that it was *after all your choice.*

He pushed my limits to engage in situations I didn't feel comfortable about, but he called me a prude, laughed at my naivety, or begged me while assuring me that 'he would never ask this' if he didn't love me this much. Then it ended up being called a slut for a sexual act that took place in a car—that he begged me for. Or threatening to tell everyone about us having sex in public spaces—because only someone promiscuous would do such a thing. He was testing my limits, then condemned me for doing it, making me pay the price for it multiple fold.

Healthy sexuality is about connection, about communication, about bonding. It should never contain an element of control, mind games, manipulation. It should never make you feel uncomfortable. It should never be used against you. **It should never be abusive.**

177

They need you for their own motives. They need you for validation. They need you for their pleasure. They need you to be able to have power over you. And their sex play is the strongest.

They master conversation, but it's a means to an end—to sex. They feign empathy, for sex. They shower you with love, for sex. They are good at it—and they won't stop at anything to get what they want.

You can have the best sex of your life, yet eventually it will leave you abused and depleted.

You might stay because of the sex.

You might stay because you believe that sex means love.

You might stay because they promised you love you've never had before.

You know you should get out, but you stay even when it's not good for you. *You see red flags.* You see your boundaries being washed away. You allow hurt. And they keep you hooked with a powerful drug—you get addicted to their love and the sex they give. Even if they hurt you in ways no one else did.

You will see it eventually. You will see through their games. And you can get out. You will heal and you will get your power back.

But it has to end. If they leave, let them. If you can, run. Even if the sex is love and the love is sex. For you, sex is connection—for them a way to rule you.

Run. Hide. Never look back. You deserve more than that.

And as impossible as it sounds, you can leave the best sex of your life behind—for your sanity.

The Narcissist's Harem of Other Women

Thinking about the other woman, a seductress in black lingerie with Russian Red lips comes to mind, who arrives and enters like a hurricane, wrecks the home, the family, to get what she needs—which is to seduce and make crazy love to the innocent husband who was mesmerised and stunned by this unstoppable force of nature.

We rarely talk about how it is the husband who is the homewrecker, how it could be him seducing another one—neglecting the needs of his official significant other, his kids and his family. We rarely talk about how the other woman is sometimes the victim, how she might not even know about what she got herself into. And there is one more rarely noted phenomenon that deserves an honourable mention: *the harem of other women of the narcissist.*

It was quite early into the relationship when I learnt that I am not only the *other* woman, I am one of the other women. His official girlfriend was waiting for him with a warm supper, while I was first blissfully unaware of being a second option, then soon I became the first of many options.

It wasn't me seducing him, it was him manipulating me into believing how miserable he was at home, how he was going to break up with his girlfriend, how he found the love of his life: me.

I can't stop wondering how many other women heard similar verbiage and whether it sounded perfect and genuine because he practised saying them so many times, that even he believed his own words.

My almost fatal collision with the narcissist started as bliss, the promise of eternity, the too-good-to-be-true perfect picture of riding away together into the sunset.

Living with the narcissist and being his primary target can be toxic in many ways: it can be abusive mentally, verbally and sometimes physically, sexually and even financially. It might take you months or years to realize what you got yourself into, it can take an eternity to figure out that they would never change, because change is uncomfortable. *But being the other woman for a narcissist is equally dangerous.*

You know that you are the other woman and he uses that against you

You knew what you signed up for, he told you early on, or you learn it soon enough. If you stay, and you probably stay, mesmerised by his charm, his words and the sex play that he is so good at, he will have no qualms telling you about all the other women, boasting about them, comparing you to them. The comparison is the first manipulation: there can be others, but you are special in one sense or the other.

Yes, there are others, but...

"I keep coming back to you..."

"We are soulmates."

"No matter how it ends, we will always be friends."

"We are connected on levels I never connect with anyone."

"I thought it was going to be just about sex, but I am falling for you."

As you are the other woman, your feelings are invalid

You don't have the right to ask about his whereabouts, you can't complain if he disappears for days—probably sleeping with someone else. You can't question him why he ghosted you, you can't tell him how it hurt you—unless you want to be ridiculed or shut up with a feeble excuse that has no solid ground.

It doesn't matter if he promised something and then he doesn't deliver. It's no surprise that he is interpreting your connection in a different way—it means everything for him until you are reeled in, and then suddenly when it starts to matter to you, he's gone—without a word.

You should just accept it and smile—you knew you were one of many, he told you in so many ways. He also told you that you are special. And out of the two conflicting pieces of information you chose to believe that you are special, because who doesn't want to be *that special someone*. The fact that he knew so many women (he told you) makes your 'being special' even more special. After all, being one and special is inferior to being special among hundreds of other women.

He is in it for the hunt

You agree that it would be casual. Just sex and talks and laughs. Of course, what else, he has his girlfriend at home. Or he is coming out from a breakup. Or something else that makes it justifiable to keep it casual.

You are in it only for sex and sex talks—and it stops being enough for him. Until you can distance yourself from him, until he doesn't fully devour you in whole, until you can keep it casual—he won't stop.

183

He'll manipulate and lodge himself into your heart, get under your skin and play mind games to confuse you to a point where you don't even remember where you were heading and the only solid point in your universe is him.

He is in it for the thrill of the chase. You recognised a red flag and you want to leave—oh no, you can't. Not under his watch. *And he is watching!*

You as a person don't matter

At first, it's all about you. Everything about you is amazing. The way you would fart would make him adore you. He adores you for being you, praises you for your unique personality, for your looks, for your style, your choice of books and music, your choice of words. You are a walking miracle he can't stop worshipping. Does it raise red flags? Hell yeah! Do you ignore them? Mostly yes.

And then when you are appropriately into him and you say so, you let him know he has power over you, that's when he stops caring. You as a person don't matter. You can go through the nastiest divorce, suffer from a terminal illness, you can be happy about a job promotion, a trip overseas, or you can be devastated by the loss of a parent—it doesn't matter. In a split second he will direct back the conversation to himself, as nothing and no one else matters.

You can try to be the empathetic *girlfriend or lover or whatever label he gives,* showing him your appreciation, caring about him—he will bathe in it

184

and he will even thank you for it. He will accept your admiration, but he will stop reciprocating it once you care enough. There is never a point where you can stop admiring him or count on his love; it is a period of constant expectations that are never returned.

He never asks how you feel, what you do, what you want. He never asks, because it doesn't matter. Your being special was only for the time until he secured you as a source of energy that feeds his empty soul.

It's all for show

The narcissist is a broken, vulnerable little animal with a void the size of Texas in his soul. He needs to fill this void with bragging and boasting, speaking about sex and women. He craves external validation in any form because his life depends on it. Without the healthy system of internal validation, he is empty, and this emptiness hurts him more than you can imagine. The world is his playground with the rest of it as pawns and puppets that he drags with him in his carefully orchestrated show.

He looks at people and all he sees is how they will validate him, how they will help him, praise him, adore him. He becomes the wildest dream of his victim(s)—the expert actor who never confuses his women, he will always give you what he can most manipulate you with.

I wanted to feel special and unique, *I wanted him to fall for me*. I got it. Those who wanted only sex, they got that. Others needed friendship, and they were promised the closest connection ever, spiced with some erotica to make it so confusing that they forgot to look for the emergency exit.

But, on the plus side. Being in the harem of a narcissist, I got to know empowered, strong, beautiful women—the other *'other'* women. They weren't competition, they were allies. We were in it together, suffering together. And no matter how we were positioned against each other (triangulation), once we saw through him, he had no power over any of us.

What if I Am The Narcissist and Not the Victim?

When I realized that I was in a relationship with a narcissist, I started to read a lot about narcissistic personality disorder. I devoured books and articles—to find some meaning in the chaos that I experienced, to find explanations where there were none and to confirm that I am not crazy.

But, just like medical students who suffer from severe hypochondria, diagnosing themselves with all sorts of illnesses that they are learning about, I caught myself finding a lot of narcissistic traits in my otherwise normal personality.

I already knew that something was off in my relationship. I knew that we were both suffering. I knew that I was suffering. But everything I read made me start to doubt myself.

What if I am the narcissistic one, and not him? What if the problem lies with me and the responsibility lies with me? What if we are both in this turmoil?

It was quite disturbing to consider that I may have changed into someone I never wanted to be. I felt I was selfish—because I was told that I was selfish, not caring about his needs. I was told that I was abusive—when I was trying to have two-way communication and I wanted to express my opinions. I felt that I was a terrible person, who always wants attention, who is clingy, demanding and impossible to satisfy.

And it was true. I wanted the attention that he used to give me, but he decided to take it away to punish me, only to show me random glimpses of affection as breadcrumbs. In other words, I was being fed tiny pieces of love and affection that left me unsatisfied. I started to become selfish, and I tried to get him to care about me too—instead of always dealing with his problems.

It is quite common that victims of narcissistic abuse start to question themselves, whether they are the narcissistic one or is it their partner. If you have to ask yourself whether you are narcissistic or not, most likely you are not.

Narcissists Don't Worry About Being Narcissistic

If you have the capability to self-reflect on this question, chances are that you are not narcissistic. Narcissists usually don't have a problem being labelled narcissistic, as they find it justifiable that they are entitled to more things than the majority of the population. Entitlement and superiority are not negative traits in their minds.

They lack empathy so they don't care if their behaviour is disturbing or abusive towards others. They don't even acknowledge being abusive or aggressive, as others' feelings don't matter to them unless they serve them some way.

Projected Traits

Narcissists are great at shifting the blame from themselves and they usually do it by projecting their negative traits onto you. If you hear from them that you are selfish, it is most likely that they are selfish. If you are labelled clingy or abusive, it speaks volumes about their co-dependency and aggressive behaviour.

By projection they accomplish two things at once: they dismiss all responsibility for their behaviour, and they make you feel terrible about yourself.

If you've been exposed to narcissistic abuse for a long enough time, your conditioning has already taught you to take the blame, to self-destruct and to apologise for everything—even for things you haven't done. Any blame-shifting confirms the victim's distorted belief that they have done something wrong—and that they are responsible for the traumatic relationship.

You are manipulated into believing that there is something wrong with you, that you are crazy, irresponsible and narcissistic. It encroaches your lower self-esteem and makes you doubt yourself.

Deserving of Abuse

Victims of narcissists are made to believe that they deserved the treatment they received. They are told so, and as they tend to do a lot of self-reflection anyway, looking for answers and explanations, there is usually no reasonable explanation for the narcissist's behaviour. Therefore, they need to find something to cling to. As they are human, they start to attribute the reasons for the abuse to our own human flaws.

"I must have done something to anger him," they may say.

As there is no other reason besides their own behaviour, they tend to believe what the narcissist is projecting—as it sounds logical. We believe that we provoked them, angered them, annoyed them, just by our very existence. We start to believe—and they say so—that we deserve the abusive treatment, and we should become better.

Human flaws are natural. They are part of our character. And while there is always room for improvement, no character flaw entitles anyone to abuse you. You don't need to change or get better— *it is the abuser who needs to stop the abuse.*

Reacting to Abuse is a Vicious Circle

It is near-impossible to not react to abusive behaviour. Especially in the beginning when it catches you off-guard and you are not yet conditioned to tone yourself down. Your disappointment, your anger and your outrage are all justified reactions that will be used against you.

A person can be yelling at you for weeks—but when you yell back once it will be brought up time again and again, painting a picture of you as an aggressive, undisciplined, impatient person, who cannot communicate assertively; making you responsible for everything bad within the relationship.

And as your expectation is different from what they make you do—such as believing in calm and assertive communication—despite the blatant double standards you will start to believe that you went too far this time, therefore you deserve their treatment.

Gaslighting You into Narcissism

The narcissist knows about their narcissism—and they use this against you at every possible turn. They know that you are empathetic. This is probably one of the main reasons that they spend time with you.

They know that you are willing to change and adapt, and they abuse your kindness.

They will call you crazy—listing all the events when you tried to speak up for yourself. They will make you question your own memory and sanity, distorting the past and pretending it didn't even happen.

They lie about what they said, and they do it so effectively that you start to doubt yourself. This is when it is extremely easy to tell you that you are narcissistic and that you are to blame for everything that happens.

The Checklist

If you find yourself wondering whether you are narcissistic or not, ask yourself the following questions:

- Do you care about others without a hidden agenda?
- Does the wellbeing of another person matter to you?
- When you self-reflect do you do it to justify what you did or to alter the course in case it's harmful to others?

If your answers are mainly **yes**, you have nothing to worry about. You are sane and caring.

Now have a look at the following questions:

- Does this ever happen with anyone but them?

- Has anyone else ever called you crazy, selfish, entitled?
- Do you usually have trouble remembering what you said if you are with anyone else?
- Do you act "crazy" anywhere else but within this relationship?

Chances are that you will answer **no** to these questions. This means that you are not narcissistic, you are just made to believe that you are. You exist also outside of this relationship and that person is the real you—without their reality being distorted deliberately.

5. BREAKING UP WITH THE NARCISSIST

Breaking The Cycle

In any toxic, narcissistic, psychopathic or abusive relationship, there is only one way out. Breakups will always hurt, you don't need to be in a toxic relationship for that, but with someone with a narcissistic personality disorder, the relationship is messy, and the breakup is even messier.

It will hurt—and you might feel that you are not ready to leave the promise of a relationship behind. In any relationship there may be points when you need to consider whether to leave or fight for the relationship. In a regular relationship, trying to figure out how to grow together, how to make compromises, how to resolve conflicts are natural. When it comes to two adult people the misunderstandings can be discussed, the passion can be reignited, the problems can be solved together. It takes two people—**it should never be the emotional labour of just one party**.

But with the narcissist, anything that questions their behaviour, any change, any compromise *is unacceptable for them.* They don't want to change, because the way of life they have created for themselves is too comfortable. They won't genuinely want to work on problems because they are the ones creating them in the first place. They don't want to discuss how they have wronged you, because in their minds you have deserved it—for they are superior and deserving of anything they want. *Your feelings don't matter. Your needs don't matter. You don't matter.*

You are nothing but a provider of fuel for them—not a person with emotions and pain. You have one purpose and that is to serve them.

If you decide that you need attention and care, if you bring up that you have needs too, they will get angry, hurt and may start to blame you for being clingy, needy and irrational. This is not how it should be—and deep down you know it.

The abusive cycle never stops because its dynamics feed them with the energy they crave. They won't stop on their terms, *it has to be you breaking the cycle*, taking away their energy and power.

You can't have a healthy, nurturing relationship with them because they don't want to give that to you. They are the centre of their own world; you can't have a place there.

The promise of that charming person who you fell in love with was an illusion. They don't have bad days and good days—this is how they are. The image you saw first was the mask, and the ugly truth behind it is the reality. They can go back to acting nicely temporarily, but it's not sustainable, because it's not who they are. The person who is worthy of your love doesn't exist, it's just a perfectly crafted shadow, a false self. They are actors—very good ones too. But when they come off the stage, their true self is unattractive, and neither charming nor funny. They are mean, bored and vindictive. They are petty and jealous. Their real self is empty—but they have the capacity of wearing different masks to make you believe that they are worthy.

One of the most difficult things is to believe that they are not broken, and you can't fix them. It's not your job to save anyone, and even if you want to, the narcissist is the worst test-subject you can choose. *They can't be saved because they don't want to be saved.*

They don't love you and they don't love themselves either. The concept of love, caring and selflessness is unknown to them—they don't understand it and they don't believe they should try to understand it.

You need to grow and heal—and you can only do this if they are not around to drag you down and hurt you again.

You have to break the cycle and stop giving them what they need.

You need to leave and never look back.

You need to stop giving them another "second chance".

You need to leave without telling them about it-to avoid it at all costs, that they lure you back in.

You need to increase your awareness about narcissistic abuse with the help of a specialised therapist and support groups.

You need to be prepared for the worst—hoovering, slandering and revenge to the fullest. Being ignorant about it can hurt you more than knowing the steps forward.

You need to reconnect with your previous life, your friends and family. Look for their support-you will need it.

You need to make sure that once you leave, you stay away.

You need a healthy distance to break the trauma bond.

You must go and avoid contact—that starts from blocking them on every possible surface, avoiding bumping into them, to the most extreme measure of changing jobs and residence. The ultimate 'no contact' comes when you can purge them from your thoughts too—but that takes a lot of time. Ignoring them on social media is an excellent place to start.

Grieve your relationship. Allow yourself to be heartbroken. The fact that they lied doesn't mean that your love wasn't real. Practice self-care and give yourself as much time you need, don't rush into anything, don't look for a rebound.

And don't blame yourself. It was never your fault.

Abuse is Abuse

When it comes to abusive people, be it just an average abuser, a narcissist or a psychopath, there are always excuses. The list of blame is endless, and they can get very creative at explaining their behaviour.

They can blame it on stress and external conflicts, substances, drugs, alcohol. They can blame it on money problems. They can blame the weather—come rain or shine. They can blame too little or too much sleep. And they can blame their victims for triggering them, for behaving in a way that they couldn't tolerate.

Not all abuse is physical—but while it is very hard to find another explanation for a black eye or bruises, it is easier to let slip other types of abuse. Name-calling, belittling, mocking you for your values is verbal abuse. Ignoring your needs and manipulating you into risqué sex, talking you into consent is sexual abuse. Gaslighting you, altering your reality and making you believe that you are crazy for calling them out on their wrongdoings is mental abuse. Just because someone never hits you, they can still abuse you and make you miserable in different ways, including verbal, psychological and sexual abuse.

Whether someone is abusive in a physical, verbal, emotional, mental, sexual or financial way—the fact remains, *it is abuse.*

And the abuse as such is never the victim's fault. We are too quick to judge someone who falls prey to an abuser, claiming that they invited the abusive behaviour, that they chose to stay, that they might have triggered them.

In our advanced society, we are adults, responsible for our own behaviour. We are supposed to manage our temper, we are supposed to deal with criticism, we are supposed to handle our conflict in an adult way. And that doesn't allow any kind of abusive behaviour.

Our society however doesn't punish all abusive behaviour and some of our patriarchal beliefs are further fuelling maladaptive coping mechanisms.

It's important to understand that if you feel that you are abused, you probably are. You are not overreacting. You are not hysterical. You are not crazy.

The narcissistic tactics will make you feel that you are the one who is too sensitive, who can't get the joke, who is acting out. But it's all part of the manipulation—to keep you in your place—providing them with the attention, care and fair share of drama that they crave.

If you feel that you are not in control of your own life—that's abuse. If you feel that you are put down or ridiculed for everything you say or do—that's abuse. If you cannot express your emotions without being afraid of repercussion—that's abuse. If you have to walk on eggshells to protect your partner's fragile ego—that's abuse.

Abuse has a million faces, but none of them should be tolerated. You deserve to be seen, heard and understood. Your needs are important, and your expectations of a decent partner are valid.

The fact that you don't leave, that you stay, that you put up with it is no invitation for abuse—*there is no valid excuse for abuse*. Not mental illness. Not addiction. Not a bad day.

If you suspect that you are victim to abuse and you have already tried to reason with your abuser and it doesn't stop, then you need to figure out how you can break the cycle, how you can leave. Because you have to leave. The best time would have been yesterday—the second best is today.

How to Break Up With the Narcissist?

There are several unforgettable milestones in a narcissistic relationship. The first kiss might be a mind-blowing once-in-a-lifetime event that renders you speechless. The first time they stonewall you or discard you might be the worst night or week of your life—until they come back pretending it never happened. The moment when you realize that you can't come up with any more excuses and you have to face the truth: they are using and abusing you, is probably more devastating than anything they say or do.

And then it starts. Your world starts crumbling down on you, you're questioning your own sanity, your feelings become shaky and invalid, you enter into a state of permanent fear and misery, terrified of what will come next.

Eventually, the moment comes. You read enough about it. You think too much about it. You care way too much about them despite everything they do to you. And you finally realize that it all happens according to a pattern.

You realize that you're probably not the only one suffering from it. You notice the subtle clues that suggest the next episode—and it works like clockwork.

The narcissist is the master manipulator, yet they work according to a certain pattern that's quite easy to pick up.

You try to change them. You negotiate. You cry and yell and give ultimatums. It works and then it doesn't.

You need to end this. Once and for all. But it's not that easy. In fact, it's the most difficult thing you ever need to do.

They Don't Want You to Leave

As long as you are providing them with what they want, they don't want to leave, and they don't want you to leave either. No matter how you feel about it, if you feel miserable, it's likely very comfortable for them.

They are doing exactly what they want. They will discard you and then come back. They might be cheating on you, looking for additional supplies, or they will just sit back and do nothing, watching you scurrying around them in a frenzy.

They are attached to you—for all the wrong reasons. It's comfortable to have you around, to be loved by you and needed by you, so why would they change it? It's perfect for them.

The Danger of Leaving an Abusive Person

If you look at the statistics of domestic violence, **a frightening number of homicide cases happen after the break-up**—for that's when the abusers lose their power over their victims and, being out of options, resort to horrendous acts.

When I was trying to get out of my abusive relationship, the support line I called suggested I lay low and make sure we are safe, not to anger him, not to provoke him—as the facts I told the support service about him positioned him at a very high level on the abusive scale.

It can be even life-threatening to try to break up with an abusive person-and in most cases, the feeling of empowerment is just simply not worth the risk of being hurt.

Get Them Leave You

Sometimes the only way is to get them to leave you.

Heartbreak and breakups hurt like hell. When you love someone toxic, it's even more difficult to part ways for they won't let you have your way. You can't just discuss it and part in peace. It has to be messy and dramatic. It has to be on their terms. In other words, *you need to become useless for them to leave you alone.*

There are a few explanations for the narcissist's behaviour. Some call it narcissistic supply, some call it fuel-that's what they are after, and anything that you do, feel, every fit you throw, every tear you shed, proves their worth.

In my books, it all boils down to energy. They crave the energy that comes from feelings, devotion and even from anger. No matter if it's positive or negative, you need to feel something and express those feelings to make them feel alive.

Your usefulness comes from the energy they take from you. Your love fuels them just as much as your resentment. Your disappointment makes them happy just as much as your passion and happiness. As long as you're not indifferent, you are giving them what they want and need.

And how could you be indifferent while they keep dragging you with themselves on an emotional roller coaster?

Get Off the Roller Coaster

When you realize—when you finally make peace with the fact that they won't change and it's not going to get any better—*you need to get out.*

The most empowering way would be to pack your bags, leave and never come back. It's not only difficult, but it can also be downright dangerous. After all, with leaving, you are about to take away the source of energy they live off. They are not going to let you.

First of all, if they realize you want to leave, they will do anything to secure you again. The honeymoon phase and the love-bombing start again and they make you forget that you ever wanted to get away. How could you leave your soul mate, the one person who gets you and loves you more than anyone ever will?

You are sucked back into the emotional turmoil until you are once again cross-eyed from lust and love. This is what they call 'hoovering'. It doesn't last longer than it has to, just to reel you in again, and then eventually everything goes back to how it was-the callous, uncaring and mean person you wanted to leave reappears. You are the one suffering in the end.

If that doesn't work, they unleash their anger. There is no such thing as "too far" when it comes to punishing you for your ungrateful behaviour. They will slander you, they will try everything to make your life a living hell. They will use everything you have ever told them against you. They will gaslight you and ruin you in any possible way.

Remember, they are after energy, so your misery and suffering will do that too.

Become Useless

To save yourself from danger, you need to withdraw the energy you used to give them so that they become the one moving on. It's not immediate, but it's effective and it can mean that you get away for good.

Understanding what they are after is the way to the blissful indifference that will save you. They want love, care, passion, anger, hatred, tears and pain. Stop fuelling their egos.

Stop displaying your affection. Stop telling them you love them or miss them.

Stop trying to change them. Stop reminding them how good they used to be and how happy you used to be with them. Stop the memory lane trip.

Stop trying to please them, don't do them favours, don't help them in any way. Did you make the coffee? Stop doing that. Did you text them from work? **Don't do it anymore.**

1. Stop engaging in their circular conversations.

They are very good at creating drama just by words, provoking you and manipulating you into an argument even if you initially agreed. Stop listening to them. Don't argue. Let their word salad slip, it doesn't matter anyway. The conversation that they are pulling you into is not about you. *It's an internal monologue in which they are using you as a puppet.* Your opinions are not going to be heard or considered. Your words won't even reach them.

2. Stop listening to them.

They don't talk to you; they talk at you—and it's always about them. How they are hurt, what they think, what they want. In their hellish monologues they will do whatever it takes to dismiss you and belittle you. You need to stop listening to them—you have probably heard it already. They won't say anything new; they won't say anything interesting. It's not a conversation, it's a means to confuse you.

3. Walk away when they provoke you.

When it comes to any kind of interaction with them, they will do anything and everything to get a reaction from you. It is to assure that you either admire and praise them or you get angry at them. Both work for them, as long as you provide them the energy they need. If you stop interacting with them when they want you to, that means you are robbing them of the power they want to have over you. Everything has to happen on their terms, that's the proof for them that they are in control. It's very difficult, because they can be very persistent, and

212

nothing is off-limits. Just learn to walk away and ignore their attempts to get under your skin. Tell them you don't have time for this and *move out of their way.*

4. Start to spend time away from them to rebuild your mental clarity.

When you are in their physical proximity, they have the chance to have an impact on you. They will keep talking to you and gaslighting you. They will make you question your own sanity. If you remove yourself from their physical proximity—even for a short time—you gain clarity and you can spend time with yourself. You can reset your priorities and find little moments that you can enjoy—without their influence. The more time you spend away and dealing with your own things the more you will see how distorted their thinking is and how they manipulated you in every area of your life. If you can, get away from them, do something you enjoy, meet friends who lift you up, go for a long walk or for a run. Clear your head and gather your strength.

5. Answer with short, factual, uninterested sentences.

If you must talk with them, try to get involved as little as possible. Don't show interest anymore, don't share your opinion. What's even more important, don't share anything personal about yourself anymore. You must know by now already that anything you say will be used against you in a future conversation. If you share your issues with your boss, you can be sure that in a forthcoming conversation it will be cited to prove how impossible a person you are. If you tell a story from your childhood, they will tweak it so they can show you how crazy you were already from an early age. If you must, talk about your boring life. If you have to have a conversation, choose a topic that bores them. Grocery shopping, nappies and your work should do. And don't let them direct the conversation back to them.

6. Be absent during sex.

Sex is one of the powerplays they use. Be indifferent. Be distant. Never initiate and try to get out of it as much as it is possible. Saying no might not be the best option because that causes rage and with some abusers you don't want them to get angry with you. But if you take away the power of sex, not caring about their bravado and self-admiration then it gets easier to separate sex from love and love from sex. You will realize that sex is their only love language and if they can't manipulate you with it anymore it's a good shield for you to be protected later on, when they want to seduce you again in a hoover-campaign.

7. Don't react when they hurt you.

They *will* hurt you. This is who they are. It's not personal, but they have the ability to make you feel as if you have been attacked. It's tough not to get defensive but try anyway. Repeat it as a mantra in your head that you know exactly why they are doing it and let it go. *It's not you, it's them.*

Leave, and Never Look Back

No matter what you do, you need to make sure that you are safe. You are your only responsibility and you need to do whatever it takes to live a full life—without letting anyone hurt you deliberately.

It might sound that you become just as bad as they are, as instead of leaving in a clear and decent way, with straightforward communication, you choose to follow their tactics and you as well choose to manipulate.

The only way is out, and you cannot be too picky about the method you choose to assure your own safety.

Besides, getting away is just the first step, you also need to stay away, which means resisting them if they want to hoover you (attempting to get you back with love-bombing), and you need to have 'no contact' to avoid further harm.

This is the first and most important step towards your new life—it won't be easy, but it is worth it in the long run.

You might need to move, you might need to change your job, you might need to unfriend your friends that might know them. You might need to change your phone number, your email address and retract completely from social media.

You might need to give up a lot of things to get your life back and it will be difficult.

Your physical safety is more important than anything. If you have kids, their safety is even more important. You might need to go to the police and report them. You might need to have a safety bag prepared, left at a trusted friend or relative. You might need to have money that they don't know about. You might get into a position when you need to escape and run for your life. All of these measures sound like extraordinary work for something that may not happen, but this is your life we are talking about, and if you stay in the relationship, it's just a matter of time before something happens.

When my head was clear enough to leave, I was preparing for it for months. I had an apartment, I had a new job, I was willing to change all my phones and other access points. I blocked him everywhere.

I moved out of the flat in full secret. One day we were there and the next there was just an empty flat.

He went crazy. He became violent. He threw fits and sent me threatening emails. He promised to hunt me down. I had never been so afraid in my life. I left my life behind me to get away from him.

He found me again—and it was difficult to get away. Thankfully he left the country eventually, when he realized we had nothing to do with each other. He stalked me online and in real life too. He followed me around. He followed my kids.

I refused to engage in any kind of conversation with him, but he still found a way to make my life a living hell—with revenge porn and slander. I needed to change jobs again to avoid the humiliation. I needed to file another police report, going through a full-scale victim-blaming process of an investigation. I had to watch how the authorities did nothing to find him and bring me justice.

But I was becoming free.

And it was because I kept a very strict no contact policy with him.

How to Go No Contact

Originally the 'no contact' rule was made up by dating coaches who suggested no contact as a means of getting back with your ex. As if manipulating someone into wanting to be with you after they left you would *really* be a viable option for most of us. As if something utterly broken could be repaired by playing hot and cold; where the coolness of pulling away would be met with the warm breeze of reconciliation.

I'm not saying it never works—some might need a wake-up call to realize how much they lost. But in most cases, it doesn't.

No matter what kind of ideology or pseudoscience, it's still manipulation and it doesn't work. It's just not how it should be. There is usually a good reason that a relationship goes south, and in most cases, the breakup comes after you tried to solve your problems in a mature way.

In this case, manipulation is not the answer. But no contact shouldn't be about manipulation. **It is about self-preservation and survival, and it's not selfish, but a necessary act.**

What Is No Contact?

No contact is nothing but a coping mechanism after a tumultuous or abusive relationship, where you allow yourself enough time and distance to heal, without being influenced by reminiscing about the relationship.

It is a harsh but effective method that can speed up the grieving process in some cases. And when it comes to breaking the trauma bond with a narcissist or psychopath, this might be the only method that works.

Why Should You Go No Contact?

In any kind of abusive relationship, you are subject to a cyclical pattern of good and bad periods. The narcissistic cycle fits perfectly into the general abuse cycle where the honeymoon phase (love-bombing) is followed by a build-up of tension (devalue), then an abusive event (discard), which will be followed by an apology and a honeymoon phase again (hoovering and love-bombing).

This is the intermittent reinforcement that is very hard to break away from.

You are conditioned to accept very little positive affirmation and, in the hope of things getting better, you also accept the abusive behaviour. It all goes according to a pattern, and the toxic partner is manipulating your emotions and keeping you close so they can use you for their needs and wants.

When you are near them, even if you already realized that you're being abused, it's near impossible to break out from the cycle—you need distance, time and clarity to break out from the trauma bond, to break the dopamine loop they expose you to and to find your way back to yourself.

What Does No Contact Really Mean?

It means that you remove yourself from harm's way once and for all, and you never look back. It means that you break all ties with them, burn each and every bridge—with no contact at all.

It's not easy and there is a lot more to it than simply just not meeting them. Most people fail with no contact, because they think that no contact is reserved for limiting or eliminating physical contact, but it's much more than that.

The point of no contact serves two objectives:

1. You gain clarity via physical and emotional distance and you gain the ability again to see your life in an objective and factual way—without your

partner distorting your way of thinking by manipulation, hoovering or gaslighting.

2. You take your partner out of the equation, making it impossible for them to intervene with your daily life, to change your mind or make you second-guess your decision.

The Obvious Parts of No Contact

There are a few points that are self-explanatory when it comes to no contact, and they are the easiest to keep on track:

- Don't meet them.
- Don't talk to them on the phone. That means don't call them and don't take their calls either.
- Don't message them. Don't accept messages from them—of any kind.

These sound very basic and as much as they seem to be obvious, they're quite easy to break.

For one, while you're under their spell, it's very difficult to resist the temptation. But please hold on. The dopamine haze will go, the withdrawal symptoms of your love will pass—you will survive it, I promise.

On the other hand, it's also difficult because they might not want you to leave, which means they will do anything to get you back or to stalk you and harass you—depending on their level of illness and the blow to their ego that comes from you leaving.

These above elements might need to be additionally complemented by the following acts:

- Blocking their number. (Or eventually changing your number)
- Blocking them on social media. *Everywhere.*
- Unfriending and blocking their family and friends, even if you were friends too.
- Changing housing so they cannot find you.
- Changing your workplace so they cannot find you.

The Less Obvious Parts of No Contact

No contact is not only about hiding and running. It is also about healing and allowing you a safe space to grow. Which means you need to stop thinking about them. You need to get to the point where you become indifferent—and the quickest way is to pretend that the whole relationship didn't happen.

You might say this is cruel since you could have invested years or even decades of your life into that relationship—but what really matters here is how quickly you can get back to yourself and not add further years to the healing process by hindering yourself.

Don't go to places that remind you of them.

Avoid your favourite bar and the restaurant that might evoke memories. Don't go near the park where you first kissed or where they asked you to marry them. They might hang around those places, hoping you'll show up, and when you do, they will do anything to get you back or hurt you.

Don't drive by their house or workplace to see them.

They will expect you to, and it won't help you move on. The sight of them will just drag you back again.

Don't hang with friends who might still be talking about them.

Nothing is sacred for them, so they will try to get you back or humiliate you with the help of friends. Imagine that everyone around them might not know that they are abusive, as they never got close enough to reveal their true selves. The friends and acquaintances that are still under their spell are like flying monkeys[9] and they will act as their lieutenants to try and help them get you back or hurt you—depending on their masterplan.

Don't stalk their social media profiles.

Even if they don't know, *you* will know, and you will see how they are living their lives without you. If they want you back, they will expect you to do so, so they will try to send you messages on their own profiles, reminding you of them.

Don't keep and look at objects and photos that remind you of them.

It might sound too harsh to throw out wedding rings and whole photo albums, but trust me, it's for the best. You don't need them anymore, so why torture yourself with things that won't lead anywhere. Throw away everything that might trigger you—I promise that there won't be a time when you'll be sorry you did it. *It's not your life anymore, so stop living in the past.*

Don't listen to music you used to listen to with them.

Music and smells are two of the most powerful psychological triggers. Stop subjecting yourself to emotions you are not yet ready to process. Delete that Spotify playlist, get rid of those files, throw away those CD's, sell the vinyl. You don't want to change your mind, so they can all go. You can't avoid hearing your song on the radio, but why hurt yourself deliberately?

It's difficult to get out, I know it is. *But once you are out, stay away.* That's even more difficult.

According to statistics[10], it takes an average of 7 times of going back and forth before the victim can finally get rid of their abuser. You need to be resilient and cold as ice. Your life might depend on it—or at least your healing and wellbeing for a long time.

Don't sabotage the healing process by exposing yourself to things that you can avoid. It's not going to be easy. It might be the hardest thing you'll ever need to do. But it's going to be worth it. I promise.

Life is amazing once you get past this chaos. So, stay strong. You can do it.

6. LIFE AFTER THE NARCISSIST

The Abyss of Victim-Blaming

People judge people too quickly. And they will blame victims for not seeing their situation, for not walking away, for not protecting themselves. Friends will blame you—or question you. Family members will stand and shake their heads in disbelief. Other women will stop empathising—pushing the blame on you, *as a victim.*

The sentence I heard too many times when it came to finding some reason for being abused, was that *"it takes two to tango."*

Every relationship—good or bad—is a product of the interaction of two people. When it comes to responsible adults this is true. Relationships are based on the concept of mutual trust and respect—

and there it is true, it takes two to keep it going, it takes two to let it fail.

When it comes to relationships with toxic individuals and abusive people this concept becomes invalid. For in these cases the relationship is not about respect, it is about power and control—serving their agenda, catering for their needs, revolving around their problems instead of being mutual.

As if it wasn't enough to go through hell, there are several layers of **victim blaming** that we will face.

Society blames the victim

With full force. Sometimes openly, sometimes in a backhanded way. It's still a man's world, and this distorted world somehow forgives a man for committing unimaginable things: rape, abuse, sexual assault, etc. It is enough to look at the #metoo movement and in its wake, those who were pardoned despite the publicly known crimes they had committed. The legal system, the police, the institutions blame the victim—not overtly, but allowing specific measures and still having procedures that make victims prove their innocence—when it's not even them being on trial.

People blame the victim

Abusers do. *"She dressed up that way.", "She went there.", "She provoked them."* And strangers are still trolling, talking, commenting, and verbally abusing victims. It is too bad that friends and family do it as well. *Why did you go there? Why did you stay? Why did you allow it? Why didn't you ask for help? Why didn't you call the police?* Hearing these questions from a friend or family member is painful. Those questions strip the perpetrator from all agency and responsibility. Nothing that happened was provoked by the victim or was a result of the victim's bad decision.

Victims blame themselves

The saddest part is when victims blame themselves. As if hearing it from society and the people around wasn't enough. The endless questions go around in circles. *Could I have stopped it? When was the exact point where I made the wrong decision? What could I have done differently? Why did I stay? Why did I allow it? Do I not have self-respect? Was he right to do it? Did I make him angry? Did I provoke him?*

It takes months or even years of therapy and/or self-help to move on from the destructive belief that we were the ones at fault; I did something, wore something, said something that I shouldn't have.

There are always turning points.

There are always decisions that could have been different at that particular time. There is always a skirt that is too short when someone gets raped. There is always a sentence that makes them hit you. There is always alcohol to blame as a means of avoiding responsibility. There is always a reason for everything. And it seems that the victim, not the perpetrator, should have behaved differently, wore something else, said something different.

As Jessica Eaton, the founder of VictimFocus puts it: "When there is a terrorist attack, government, police and public figures say "we will not change our way of life, we will not change our behaviours… we will carry on as normal because we deserve a safe society." But when women are being raped and assaulted, government, police and public figures say "women, change your behaviours… do something different". Why are women supposed to change their lives and their behaviours for offenders?"[11]

Abuse, rape, sexual assault don't happen by chance. *It is a choice.* A choice made by the perpetrator. It is never right. It is never justified. So how about putting the blame right where it belongs? **It's never with the victim!**

Should I Report It or Should I Let It Go?

A frightening number of abuse, rape, and sexual assault cases go unreported. The number of reported cases is already terrifying, it is estimated that 734,630 people were raped (threatened, attempted, or completed) in the United States alone in 2018[12]; but it is clearly just the tip of the iceberg. According to recent statistics[13], 3 out of 4 cases will remain unreported due to multiple reasons.

The question is often asked... *why didn't she report it?*

Apart from victim-blaming, reporting abusive behaviour is not as simple as it seems. Victim-blaming runs deep in society, and it runs deep in people's minds. So deep, that even victims blame other victims and victims blame themselves. As part of rape culture, next to slut-shaming and body objectification, victim-blaming is definitely in the top three crimes.

Let's just stop for a second, and think about how difficult it could be for the victim to report such a case, if we try to understand the reasons—it might shine a light on the underlying causes, and help to understand better how the nature of abusive behaviour, the circumstances and societal factors can weigh in-and result in unreported cases.

So, why didn't she? What on earth could possibly stop her from seeking well-deserved justice?

Shame

Being a victim of an assault is not a crime. The assault is the crime. *Yet it's the victims who feel ashamed.* Shame for not being able to foresee it, or prevent it, or stop it. Feeling ashamed that somehow it was their fault, something they have said or done triggered the other to make the abuse possible. Shame that they played a part, that they brought in on themselves— by some or another means. They are ashamed and afraid of being humiliated for it.

Shame stops us from speaking up; shame stops us from defending ourselves; shame stops our ordinary world from functioning. Shame shatters our image of the world, and it leaves us speechless and broken. It distorts our reality to the point of questioning our sanity. It catches us off guard, and it strips us from the power we have over our lives. It paints a picture of us that we don't want to see: a terrible mirror image of our broken selves. *Shame debilitates.*

Lack of help

A lot of survivors enter the legislation system because they want to be heard, they want justice, they want it to be acknowledged that all the awful things that were done to them will be sanctioned.

Only to face the cold reality of not being heard, not being understood, not being believed.

Only to face the tragic situation that the details of the assault matter more than the fact of it. In a police investigation, above all…

What was the angle? What time was it exactly? What were you wearing? How much alcohol did you consume?

Or to face the fact that the assault does not fit into a legal category. Or to be discouraged from carrying on with the reporting of it, as the process will not come to a resolution soon enough—if at all.

Abuse is abuse; rape is rape—regardless of time, clothing, alcohol in the bloodstream, angle, etc. The legal and justice system is not ready to hear the words of the victim—sure they look for the injustice, but in doing so, they often question the victim's credibility, memory, or motives.

Many do not report because they don't trust the system enough. They think they won't be heard, listened to, believed, trusted, supported. They don't report it, as they are advised by officials not to.

Fear

Sometimes we don't report it, because we are afraid. We are scared of losing so much. Losing our love, our relationship, or losing our mind. And sometimes we are threatened to keep our mouth shut.

In a lot of cases, the assault is committed by someone we know or someone who we are still committed to. Someone we are dependent on. In cases, the assault is part of the abuse cycle's terror phase, followed up by a calm and beautiful honeymoon phase yet again, for the first or umpteenth time.

Empty threats do not feel empty when you are scared for your life. Reality cannot kick in when you are too busy covering your blackeye from your workmates and family. *Reasoning cannot touch you when survival is on the top of your list.*

Fear can stop you mid-way. Making you freeze, like a deer in the headlight; understanding the 'life or death' type of the situation, still unable to move anywhere, standing in harm's way.

Downplaying

Sometimes we don't report it because we tell ourselves that it is not even real, not that bad. Or someone else convinces us that it doesn't qualify as assault. *"Yes, he hit me, but it wasn't a real blow." "Yes, he raped me, but maybe I wasn't clear enough on saying no." "Yes, he had no right to do it but did I have the right to deny him what he wanted anyway?"*

"It wasn't really that bad. It wasn't rape; after all, he is my husband. I vowed to be with him for better or worse. I angered him, so no wonder this happened. How could I say it anyway?"

To save face, to keep the image you have of yourself, to save a relationship, to save someone who means a lot to you, to save someone who just made a mistake—**we rewrite our narrative**. Maybe we just overreacted. Perhaps we are just too sensitive. It wasn't such a big deal. We can sort it out.

But we cannot.

Love

And sometimes we don't report, because we love the one who hurt us. Because we want that person back. The one who loved us and who couldn't hurt, not really. We don't want them to get into any trouble. We don't want them to be punished. We forgive, we move on and there's no point in trying to stay away. We are meant to be.

There is always a price tag on everything, and maybe this is the price we pay for the love that we have. This is a fallacy. We think that true love prevails. If it's meant to be it will be. You don't know anyone until you know the darkest sides of them.

Love blinds us. Love makes us irrational. Love makes us defend those that we need defence from. Love makes us vulnerable and being beaten or raped is vulnerable. It is, but whoever talked about opening up to being vulnerable, surely didn't mean to be beaten-black-and-blue or ripped-their-clothes-off kind of vulnerability.

There are cases when it is impossible to report it. I am not saying that it shouldn't be reported. I am not encouraging anyone to keep silent about it. The opposite! We need to speak about it, we need to reach out for justice!

But I know that it could happen that you get trapped in a certain reality—of your own creation or someone else's—that makes it downright impossible to come out with the truth.

The bad news is, reporting abuse doesn't automatically mean redemption, justice, and peace of mind.

The good news is that healing isn't related to reporting an abusive event—we'll get there soon.

The biggest learning although, is that *forgiveness will set you free*, not punishment. After years of silence, I finally reported my abuser because I didn't want him to get away with it. Nothing happened. It didn't go anywhere. No investigation or questioning reached him. I was dragged through hell and back by legal entities and police detectives-only to relive what I wanted to forget so badly. It was all useless- and it just angered and depressed me even more.

I wanted him to be punished. Yet he didn't even get a fine.

After years of depression, anxiety, therapy, journaling, self-reflection, I realized that no punishment is going to give me back the years I lost. No sanction, fine or prison time would make up for the time and energy that he took away from me-the years he hurt me, and the time I was looking for justice.

I couldn't stop him from hurting me. The law couldn't stop him either—not during, not after. But no matter what happened or didn't happen, my life needed to go on anyway. And I needed to forgive him.. My forgiveness had nothing to do with him. What he had done was unforgivable. I still needed to forgive—for me. For the sake of my sanity. For the sake of the life that I wanted to live. And that has no room for anger, frustration or hate in it. Even though he would deserve all of it—I don't deserve any of it.

How To Take Revenge
On The Narcissist?

You have been wronged. You are hurting. You are crippled. You're lost in your sense of self and there is a myriad of emotions inside you that are impossible to process. You want to get even. You want them to hurt. You want them to feel the pain that they caused you. You want them to suffer just as much as you are suffering.

You want revenge.

You dream about it. You plan it. You spend a copious amount of time imagining how they would feel when you hurt them. You keep picturing their pain.

You want revenge because you feel that if you can make them pay for what they have done to you it will be easier to move on, to get closure and live your life. You want to show them that you are over them so much that you are ready to hurt them. You want to show that you are strong enough and they were wrong to underestimate you.

You plan it all. And then you hesitate. Because everything you can think of feels too low. It feels petty even if your plan seems grandiose and magnificent. You are confronted inside—part of you wants them to suffer and the other part knows that it's not you. You start to wonder if they changed you into a monster who now wants to manipulate and hurt others.

We are decent human beings. We inherently believe in justice. We believe that good deeds have good outcomes and bad deeds have bad consequences. We believe that goodness is a merit. We believe that life is just and fair. *We want to believe that things happen for a reason.*

Then with the narcissist, we lose it. We are faced with evil and righteousness fades into the distance. We think that the only way to beat them is to join them. And we want them to pay, to suffer, to hurt— because that would be fair.

Is it even possible to get back at them?

It is possible to get revenge on the narcissist. There are several ways, but most of them have a downside, and while they are master manipulators who don't care about others at all, you are not like them. Cruelty doesn't come naturally to you—you need to exert a lot of energy to keep up your hateful thoughts for too long.

What are the ways to legally get back at them, aiming for resolution?

1. Expose them

Once you get to know them and all the character flaws, they have, and nasty things they have done, you want the whole world to see who they really are. You want others to know who they are up against— to warn everyone who has been ever around them, even your next victim. You don't understand how others can't see them for who they are. It seems like a fair thing to do, and you might even have to do it to defend yourself.

But they are very good at putting on a show—you of all people should know it. After all, they have led you on for a long time before you first saw the façade. If you have been their primary target then the rest of the world hasn't received the same amount of evil mistreatment, it was reserved for you. Mistreatment always hurts the most to those who are the closest to them and who keep their double sided (duality) mask on with others, having the ability to trick others through sharing their positive side, which reinforces the disbelief that they could do anything wrong.

There is a chance that others wouldn't believe you and they might use your tactics against you—proving that you are crazy and unstable. Moreover, it can be downright dangerous to anger them, as they could unleash hell on you to keep up their appearance. There is also always the possibility that it may happen in a public space, shaming you further.

The best thing you can hope for is to cast doubt around them, but their retort would probably make you feel even worse.

2. Criticise or belittle them

Their world revolves around the false self they believe is them. And they are entirely incapable of taking criticism. Choosing to belittle them or criticize them sounds like a good idea—after all you just show them what it feels like to be ridiculed. It's easy too, because they take everything as a criticism—so any negative comparison, any minor put down, anything that questions them will hurt them.

But in return they will hurt you even more. And while you are a decent person who might be just pointing out their real shortcomings in a subtle way, they (most likely) will attack you with full force. Did you think they have told you everything that might hurt you? Think again. They are extremely creative and cruel—they will drag out everything you have ever said, they will point out and aggrandise your imperceptible flaws and turn around every compliment they ever told you.

Moreover, they won't understand that now, you are getting back at them, because even the slightest criticism hurts them to their core. Did you disagree with them a year ago about someone's haircut? That hurt them just as much as questioning their authority, when you boldly tell them that they are losers in all areas of their lives. They don't feel the difference in accusations or the type of accusation—because for them **hurt is hurt.**

3. Manipulate them

I'm sure that if you spent enough time with them you already know all their ways that they manipulate you with stonewalling and refusing to tell you what the problem is; silent treatments and being absent for days or even weeks; accusations of not being there for them when they needed you. Or, promising something and then doing it with someone else, cheating on you, comparing you to others and making you question your own worth through triangulation (triangulation is when they bring a third person into the relationship to maintain control. It may take different forms but it's either about creating unnecessary comparisons or to play the triangulated individuals against each other in a divide and conquer way), exposing confidential information about you to friends and pretending that it was alright, committing something against you and then blaming you for it.

You know all these, so why not do the same with them. Show them how it feels.

The problem is that manipulation is *their* second nature, not yours. They have chosen you as their victim because you are a decent person with basic human values, love, care and empathy. I would go to the extent of saying that you don't have a mean bone in your body, and you would never want to deliberately hurt anyone. You won't change your nature and inherent caring attitude towards others overnight, not even if someone hurt you, because it's not who you are. Your conscience wouldn't allow you to be hurtful on purpose. You can't ignore someone in need.

If you manipulate them, you might anger them and they will get back at you immediately—with their near-lethal artillery, if they are prepared. You hope that they recognize how heinous their behaviour is, and it would probably fall on deaf ears because they would go *into playing the victim role and blame you for hurting them*. You can't teach them about basic human values—if they could be taught, they would have already learnt it. You can't show them how hurtful they act because they justify their actions by their superiority—they are entitled to treat people as they want, but no one else can treat them the same way; therefore, they may think they are invincible.

4. Ignore them

Doing your best to ignore their manipulation tactics is one of the hardest things that you will need to do. They are experts at overt and covert abusive acts and no matter how mature and stable you are, they will find your weak spots.

The aim of the manipulation is to get a reaction from you, so in case it seems to fail, they will resort to more rude comments or severe abuse. If they are physically abusive too your lack of reaction might trigger them to go further and punish you for not responding in a way you should.

While ignoring them, you need to tread carefully and take care of yourself because it's one of the things that angers them most. Sometimes ignoring them requires manipulation from your side—which takes a lot of your energy and after a long enough time with them, *constantly walking on eggshells, you need all your energy to just survive another day with them.*

On a mental level, ignoring their acts and manipulation is a good path to go down on. You need to get to a point of indifference, where they can't hurt you anymore. It's a long journey and it takes time. Pretending you don't care is a good way to start but it, again, won't teach them anything.

5. Defy them

They say that the safest way to check whether someone is narcissistic or not is to say no to them. If they can take no as an answer, then chances that they are not narcissistic. Narcissists believe that the world is their playground and they are entitled to everyone's care and attention. It means that they can call you in the middle of the night and ask you to listen to them for hours regardless of your needs. They would ask you to drive an hour to fetch something for them, even if it's a huge sacrifice from your side. They would expect you to ditch anything and everyone so that their needs should be catered to.

As a means of revenge, it won't work, because they wouldn't notice it as revenge—just an act from you that they don't like. They would turn it against you and call out on your heartless behaviour, turning themselves into a victim. Remember, **they are great at playing the victim, they have practised it for decades.**

But saying no to their shameless requests is a good way to separate yourself from them emotionally and in case you had any doubts about their real selves this exercise will show you how they don't care about you—they care about themselves only. If you need any further proof that they are treating you wrongly, *defying them will bring you the necessary proof of how much they are using you on a daily basis.*

6. Live your best life

They say happiness is the best revenge. And it sounds so simple and it might be true. But when you are caught up in the spider web of their narcissistic abuse, thinking about happiness is the last thing on your mind.

You need to take steps towards building your best life—even if it seems unattainable from where you stand. You want instant revenge and you want to make them pay—but everything you can do will backfire and they will come out winning and grinning, *leaving you bruised and hurt.*

Living your best life means that you leave them behind, that you get to a point where they can't reach you, can't manipulate you, can't hurt you. Your best life comes after getting away and staying away. Your best life comes after you move past the trauma, after you start to remember again that you deserve love and care, after drawing and keeping your boundaries. It starts when you recognise that you are worthy of love and attention despite what they had told you. It starts when you allow others to treat you well without looking over your shoulder for monsters.

The revenge process is a slow one. And I know that this is not what you want. I've been there. But this is what you need. However, it's important to note that this is not revenge executed for the sake of it, it is part of the healing process.

You need your life back—because of the two of you, you are the only one who will ever have a life worth living, in your opinion. They won't ever change. They won't learn. They won't get better. You might think they will be different with someone else, but trust me, this is who they are, this is the only way of living that they know.

You can have a great life. You know how to love. You know what trust is. You know how to care about someone without having a hidden agenda. You have a heart, a soul and a mind that are full of beautiful facets that make you into who you are.

They are empty. They don't know how to give love and accept love. They don't know how to be happy because they never appreciate the little things that make life worth living. They can't be helped because they have never helped anyone out of the goodness of their hearts. They won't find someone who is better for them then you—because no one is good enough for them, ever. They will be forever lonely trying to fill the void by manipulating people into loving them and admiring them.

The best revenge is to move on. It's difficult. Heartbreaking. Devastating. You need to leave your present, your past together and the future they promised you. It seems too steep of a price. But life starts after them. Everything with them was merely an illusion. You will get your revenge; *you need to trust the process.*

Should You Warn Their Next Victim?

Either they left you or you left them, when the relationship is over after a huge, humiliating discard from their side or a grand escape from yours, there will be a next victim. They are probably already in the picture—either in the form of an affair or just someone they have been grooming for a while.

In many cases the narcissists have a harem of secondary supplies next to their primary target and whether you are aware of them cheating on you or not, chances are that they will have someone to replace you with soon enough.

Even if they were the ones your narcissistic ex cheated on you with, you probably come to the question *whether you should warn them.*

In a regular breakup, if your ex finds a new partner while you are still not over them the biggest questions are: Are they better? Younger? Better looking? Better in bed? You might feel jealous and hurt, but if your ex was a half decent person, you don't think about running to their new partner warning them. After all, the love might have died, you grew apart or you are not who you believed each other to be. We all deserve happiness and it's only natural that some relationships fall apart.

With a narcissistic breakup, the scene is very different. You know what will happen. You know how it will play out with the next supply of 'victims'. Yet they seem to be over the moon, parading with their new conquest, shown how unutterably in love they are. They might even rub it into your face just to hurt you some more, how much better, prettier, younger, more desirable the new partner is—and they are probably a better person; more tolerant, not to mention madly in in love, unlike you, the clingy, needy, anxious creature.

When you are just out of a relationship with a narcissist, knowing that they will land someone else that they will abuse, **the question is whether you should warn them.**
In short, don't try to warn them.

In detail, let me tell you why not.

1. They won't believe you

The new partner is probably going through the very same process that you had been going through back when it started. They are being love bombed and now they are the new soul mate. They get all the attention and special treatment—the same that you used to get in the beginning. They are being groomed and reeled in right now.

Everything is beautiful and nothing hurts. They are in the initial stages of falling in love because the narcissist is really great at making someone fall for them.

How could they believe you that the fairy tale they find themselves in is nothing but an act? How would they believe you when they feel beautiful, appreciated, cherished? The new partner is so high on the love they feel that no rational thinking reaches them. Least from a crazy ex, like yourself. Because this is what you are. The crazy ex who couldn't appreciate them, who couldn't understand them, who was disposable and replaceable. You are a means to make the new target feel even better—in comparison to you they are the new shiny toy, the new love object, the most adorable person on earth.

If you come in with all your 'crazy' stories and claims of abuse it would be easier to believe that you were unworthy of the narcissist's love than to imagine that the love they feel is based on a lie.

They are irrational, because they are in love. They would turn on you, because you hurt the narcissist according to their stories of you—because, there are terrible stories about you, discrediting you from the beginning. Just like you used to hear stories about all the crazy exes who were terrible, obsessed and impossible to please. You wouldn't have believed them if they had wanted to warn you. Or, if you think back you might even remember someone who actually tried to warn you, but you were too caught up in the haze of love that you shrugged them off.

2. Your ex will use your warning against you

If you imagine the current setup with your ex and their new target, they are in a phase of utter bliss. They are soul mates—just like you two used to be. They are in love—even if it's fake love from the narcissist's point of view. And of course, no one on earth can understand the state that they are in. They are in isolation and they are building a life together. The world and other people can't understand them—how could they, when it's a once-in-a-lifetime love that no one else has ever experienced?

The new partner is hearing the same things as you used to and the warning would never reach them mentally.

Your ex would use it to prove that they were right to leave you, because obviously you don't deserve them, you are vindictive and petty, trying to create conflict and drama wherever you go. Of course, it didn't work out with you, your warning is the proof. And the new partner is buying into it. It is the first sign of triangulation, when at first, they are compared to you—winning it all.

They will be told that they love them precisely because they are not like you. Your character will be used to shape them. It will be proof of how to act; what the new partner should never do. You will be the perfect model for overreacting and being clingy— this will be used as a cautionary tale for the next victim in learning how not to act unless they want to end up like you, dumped and miserable.

3. You will be called crazy

Remember the crazy exes they used to tell you about? How they behaved? How they were obsessed? How they never left them alone—or so they said? At the time you were surprised how people can behave, having no dignity or manners. At the time when they were fictitious characters in the story told by your ex it all seemed surreal and you were glad they were gone.

Now you are that crazy, obsessive person they tell their stories about. You are the one who just couldn't let them go. You are the one who is making things up.

Interestingly, all the exes are crazy—including you.

Whatever you do will be used against you once you are discarded or you left them. Nothing is sacred. You will be called names. You will be called crazy. You will be called irrational. If the reality is not enough, they will come up with stories about you— after all you are nowhere to defend yourself, so they have nothing to lose.

You will be used as a puppet in their show to groom the next victim and if you provide a warning to the new partner, your claims and accusations will be dismissed, *for you are discredited already.*

4. The next victim needs to go through it

Looking back, you had to go through it on your own to believe it was possible. In the beginning you wouldn't have believed a crazy ex. You didn't believe the first acts of devaluation. You couldn't believe they could ever discard you. Then you thought they would never come back and they did.

It has been a roller coaster with lots of unexpected and unprecedented twists and turns, that you had no idea that there would be any more surprises and they had just started the process.

They changed you and they are changing their new victim as well. They made you tolerate and accept things that you have never thought you would—and even if looking back you could say that you were under their spell, this is exactly what will happen to the next person in line.

The narcissist is a master manipulator and they will guide through each victim through a tailored process—similar but not exactly the same as anyone else's. You might think you know what they are going through, but *their torture is personalised*—with eerily similar patterns yet still different.

It's a lonely journey and once you are out you need to stay out. *When your journey is over, you need to move on to healing.*

5. You are your only responsibility

When it comes to healing, you are your sole responsibility. You have enough on your plate, you have enough trauma to process and you have a whole lost future to grieve. It is only natural that you want to distract yourself and solve someone else's problem to avoid dealing with your own. But at the end of the day, you don't take responsibility for anyone else but yourself.

You don't go out of your way and make a fool of yourself to warn and save someone who doesn't want to be saved yet. You don't worry about their well-being when your own well-being is still so fragile and vulnerable. You don't go backwards, reliving the past through someone else, just because you can't yet see your own future.

Your healing process is more important than anything. **Your mental health is your responsibility. Your physical safety is your**

responsibility. Your emotions, your anger and fear are your responsibility.

You have enough to deal with, without adding an extra element—caring for someone else.

They would deserve a warning, but just like you they wouldn't have heard it neither need it. So do what you have to do. Get better. Grieve. Move on.

6. You need to move on with your own life

There is life after the narcissist. In fact, life only begins. Even if it looks hopeless and desperate. Even if it looks dark and you don't know what to do with your life anymore. You need to find the strength in yourself to move on.

And moving on involves no contact. And no contact means that you are distancing yourself completely from their life. If you do 'no contact' perfectly you wouldn't even have to know about the next victim. If your ex is blocked on social media, if you never bump into each other, if you blocked every possible surface to contact you at, then you can just assume that they found someone new **but you shouldn't know who.**

'No contact' means that you block them from your thoughts and from your life completely. This is what will make you strong enough to resist them once they try to hoover you. This is what will allow you to get back the agency that they had taken away from you. This is how you will become empowered and independent again.

Their life—including the long list of forthcoming potential victims—is not your concern anymore. You don't owe anyone anything. You don't need to take responsibility for them—those days are gone. There is no blame lying with you if you don't do anything—there is no one to blame you anymore.

Your character, your decency, your goodness is not related to how you interact with their victims—your life has nothing to do with them anymore. You don't have to be empathetic. You don't have to care. No one judges you if you walk away.

You have to walk away. You can't let anything pull you back in.

You can't keep dancing with the devil and asking why you are still in hell.

You need to get closure, often without them.

Getting Closure
On Your Own

I t's difficult to accept that you won't get any answers. It's a burden to know that you are left alone with your own thoughts with no one understanding you. It's only natural to crave for some kind of closure.

If only you knew the reason why they left. If only they told you if they stopped loving you. If only you could know at least that it was real. If there were explanations it would be easier to accept. With no closure, it seems impossible to move on.

With a narcissist, you will never get answers. You will never know why they chose you and why they chose to hurt you. You will never know if you could have done something differently or if it was doomed from the moment you met. You will never know if they really meant what they said—the good and the bad.

You are thrown in limbo—alone with your pain and there seems to be no way out.

Truth is, it is possible to move on without closure. And when you understand and accept that they work according to a certain pattern you won't need their individual explanations anymore. The narcissistic patterns are very similar, the hurt they cause is almost the same, their motivation is the same: to acquire fuel from their partner.

You cannot have done anything differently—there is no way you could have fixed them and changed them. **It's important to understand that it's not about you, even if it's you who is hurting the most.**

Know that healing is an upward spiral

At times you feel you are moving forward, you are getting better, life starts to resemble a state of normalcy… and then in a split second, it feels you are back to square one, and weeks and months of progress go down the drain. Everything feels gloomy and hopeless again, for the thousandth time. But this is not square one, and not everything went out the window, not every bit of progress is lost.

It feels as if you were thrown back yet again, but it is already a different level, a next phase of the healing spiral. And it goes on and on, moving upwards—until it starts to feel like life again.

Don't be ashamed to ask for help

Fear, shame, feeling powerless, feeling unseen, feeling unheard-they are hard to deal with even one by one. In such cases, there are usually more than just one of these playing a huge part in stopping you.

You don't need to do it alone. You can ask for help. Maybe help is not where you look for it-it is possible that legal help will not be satisfying enough, but this doesn't mean that there is no help out there.

Get help, seek therapy—any way you can. There are free therapy opportunities helping abuse victims. There are foundations assisting women in different ways-from mental, through financial, to legal support.

But this facet is important: *make sure to choose a therapist who understands the nature of abuse and assault cases.* Ensure you feel safe and unashamed. Make sure that they are on your side without you needing to get them on your side. And walk away if you don't get the help that you expected—there will be another one who gets you.

You don't need to do it alone.

Speak up and be heard

To be heard and believed is usually why victims would go to report an abuse/assault case. And sometimes it doesn't happen, and sometimes just the fear of it not happening can stop you from reaching for help. But speaking up is more important than you would think. To know it that it was not your fault, doesn't only come from the perpetrator being punished.

Support groups are great; people who went through the same stuff will surely help you. In the digital age, it is easier than ever. The support groups can be open or closed to the public and others are shrouded in secrecy. You can find closed or secret communities where you can feel safe, where you will be understood and no one will judge you.

Friends are great! They are there to have your back all the time, this is their job; this is what friendship is about. If for some reason they don't get you, or they don't get the severity of the issue, let them help you in a different way-just being there, listening to you, keeping you company is enough. And sometimes that's all you should expect.

Do you know, what's even better? To open up to strangers and receive love from them. The best is if someone unknown supports you, someone who doesn't know you and is not biased towards you, who has an objective opinion on your story and still gives you back your hope in humanity... that's the greatest feeling of all.

That is when you finally feel that the world around you falls back to its place; when you see that this world is not against you, it's back on your side. When you experience that your vulnerability is not a mistake. When you realize that weakness is a sign of strength. *When you understand that it was not your fault.*

How Can You Heal?

When you go through hell and back, when you have been chewed and spat out a hundred times, when you paid for everything that was ever committed against you—there will be a time when you will start healing. In fairness, you already started it, it just doesn't yet feel like it, but the first steps on your healing journey start when you first say no, when you first think that something is off, when you first want to fight your situation instead of being a passive bystander.

Healing is different for everyone—it's your own unique journey, where you are the protagonist and everything else falls way side. It's difficult, it's daunting, it came to be downright devastating, to try to pull yourself out of the hole you find yourself in. When you are trying to find the way back to yourself, after being wrecked by a narcissist, it seems impossible that you would ever make it back out to the light. All that you can see is darkness—around you and inside you.

But this is where you start. This is how you can build yourself up from ground zero, this is how you have enough space to think twice about which elements you want to keep and which to cast away. You have been given a clean slate—even if you never asked for it—and *at some point, it will be clear that it is a gift.*

The box full of darkness is yours. You never wanted it. But it's yours and you can decide what to do with it. You can go through it—again and again. Or you can process it and then close it for good—your experiences shape you, but they don't define you. What you learned is yours to keep.

Healing from narcissistic abuse is not linear. You need to deal with a lot of emotions along the way. Heartbreak, grief, disappointment, trust issues, emptiness, uselessness, complete loss of hope—you have a lot to cope with, and each process is not singular; in other words, they don't necessarily follow each other. They might come at you at once, dragging you down. And when you feel you just made progress and smile for the first time in a long time, it's possible that the next day will feel worse than the day before, but that is not a failure, simply a part of the healing process.

It is natural. Your mind is making space for all the things that were too terrifying to imagine or to get prepared for. Your brain adapts to the new situation (neuroplasticity) and you need to undergo changes that you never wanted. It is a slow process and at times, it feels futile. But it's not. You are healing. And eventually you will feel it too, just give it time.

To simplify the healing process, I broke it down into three main phases—not based on the emotional turmoil that goes on in your head, but on the cognitive processes that can help you make progress even when emotionally it feels that you are stuck.

- Education and Awareness
- Safe Processing
- Useful Distraction

Education and awareness

The first step towards healing is to recognise the situation where you are in. Believe it or not, this is the most difficult of all. To face yourself and admit that things have gone south and it's not your fault and not your task to fix. To be aware enough so that you could recognise abuse without trying to look for explanation or excuses. To be determined enough to want to get out of it. *To be strong enough to ask for help.*

You need to read a lot—because you need to understand it. And then you need to believe it, too. This is your life, but you can tap into the collective knowledge base of others to see how they did, how they got out, how they healed.

The previous chapters were about information and awareness, even if it's painful to see what you lost and how you were manipulated.

Safe Processing

Once you are aware enough and you know what you are up against, you need a safe place to process your thoughts and emotions. There is a lot to process and you need every help you can get.

At the same time, it is important to find helpers who understand you and who will support you on your journey without victimizing you again. Finding the right therapist is key to your future healing. Surrounding yourself with people who understand you, support you and don't question you, can help you cope in seemingly impossible situations. Although they may challenge you as part of the healing cycle, it won't be a negative process.

I will talk about therapy and support groups as ways to process your experiences under safe circumstances.

Useful Distraction

No matter how busy you used to be when you were in a relationship with the narcissist—you will realize how much time and energy they took from you when they are out of the picture. You will see how your thoughts and actions had always considered them—and now with them gone, you have too much time on your hands. You need to find useful distractions as healing methods—to break the dopamine loop of your love addiction, to get back your agency, to become independent from them once again.

For me, anger processing techniques, mindfulness, exercise and writing worked. That's what I am going to share with you.

The Importance of Finding the Right Therapist

There might come a point in your healing journey when you feel that you can't process the emotional turmoil inside your head anymore, and you need external help. Finding the right therapist when it comes to narcissistic abuse recovery is sadly not as easy as it should be.

Even without the narcissistic element, finding the therapist whose demeanour aligns with yours can be a daunting task. It is not about knowledge or professional experience; it is more about personalities. Sometimes you just don't click. And when it comes to opening yourself up and making yourself vulnerable, you are better off with someone you can trust and who you find right for you. It is a bit about interpersonal chemistry and matching temperaments. There are therapists who will work well with your personality, and others that won't be a good fit.

It is important to look for someone you can fully trust and with whom you feel comfortable. Any abuse or therapy situation is already uncomfortable, you don't need the extra discomfort coming from the lack of compatibility.

Most therapists offer trial sessions when you both can decide whether you would be a good fit—and if not, you can part ways without hard feelings. There are cases when a therapist refuses to treat you—and it's a good sign, because it means that either they are personally triggered so they can't treat you with the necessary objectivity or they don't feel confident enough in your specific area to be of help for you. And there should be cases when you say no to the therapist—no matter how much they might have been praised by others. If you feel that something is off and you sense that you won't be able to be yourself, it's time to look for another one.

When it comes to narcissistic abuse, a highly knowledgeable professional can be an invaluable support in the healing process. There are lots of counsellors and therapists who are empathetic, validating and sensitive—on the other hand, there may be professionals who don't have the appropriate information about the nature of narcissistic abuse. With a wrong approach it is easy to once again victimize an abuse survivor with seemingly harmless questions and suggestions for self-reflection.

In a lot of cases, therapy is focusing on what you can change and those are your circumstances, your perspective and your behaviour—as it is you sitting across your therapist. The only things that you can change are related to you. But in case of narcissistic abuse, asking the victim to self-reflect better, to look for reasons within, to figure out why they are hypersensitive to the attacks can contribute to further abuse.

It takes a trauma-informed expert not to misunderstand the anxiety and sensitivity of the abuse victim and not to try to get them to change or reconsider. The therapists' main job is to be empathetic, supportive and to show the right way towards self-compassion so that the victim can gain back their lost agency and power over themselves.

The right therapist will help you get to love yourself again, by validating your experiences and giving you the needed credit for your own actions. How can you recognise the right therapist?

They validate the abuse

The right therapist won't question your experiences or pain. They will validate you by recognising that you were abused, gaslit and manipulated. They won't ask you to work on your insecurities, but they will help you recognise the triggers that you have.

They understand that abuse is abuse and it is never justified. They don't question you whether you triggered your abuser, whether you did your part of the work, whether you are a good enough person not to deserve the abuse. Abuse is abuse even if it's reactive—and a good therapist will make you believe that it is not your fault.

They understand narcissism

As there is not enough professional discussion about narcissistic abuse and its covert nature makes it very difficult to analyse it. Some professionals think it is just another relationship problem to solve. Abusive relationships work differently.

But the right therapist understands it and knows how distorted the dynamics are of this type of relationship. They understand that it is a power play and a manipulation scenario without trying to shift the blame onto the victim.

You don't need to educate them about stonewalling, gaslighting and triangulation because they already know about it and educate themselves on it. You don't need to explain to them how narcissistic abuse works, and you don't spend the whole therapy session giving them lectures on power dynamics.

They will focus on the abuse, not on your part in it

As responsible people we have to take accountability for our actions and decisions. An invalidating therapist might focus on why you stayed, for by staying you are enabling the abuser and the only solution is to leave. A validating therapist knows how difficult it is to leave an abusive relationship because of trauma bonding, financial dependence or any other manipulation (suicide threats, threats about child custody etc.). They will help you in finding ways to *detach yourself* and *encourage you to leave* whenever you can.

They don't think that abuse is a relationship problem

Most relationship problems depend on two people in the relationship. If you find an invalidating therapist, they might think that you need to work on your triggers of jealousy when the real problem is that you are being manipulated, cheated on and used in triangulation.

When there is a relationship problem and both parties are willing to work on the solution and share the emotional work, it is only fair to do your share of the work. But a validating therapist understands that narcissistic abuse has nothing to do with the victim and it is entirely about the abuser.

The first step they can help you with is making you believe that you are not part of the problem and because it's still you who has to solve it, they assure you about their full support.

They don't question the manipulation

They don't look for your triggers and insecurities. They don't try to figure out how you might have brought it on yourself. They don't jump into full psychoanalysis mode to discover how your relationship with your parents had doomed you to fall victim to a narcissist. They know and confirm that you have been conned and manipulated into something that you couldn't have seen coming. *Just the mere fact that you don't need to explain that you were wronged is already a big step towards healing.*

They are empathetic instead of neutral

Some therapists believe that professional neutrality is a must—therefore they keep a neutral expression and blank face when you are telling them about your story. You need empathy and you need to see emotional reactions to feel that the abuse that you suffered was indeed severe. If the therapist doesn't show any reaction and hides behind the cold professional mask, you might feel that they are not interested, your story doesn't matter or it further spirals you into gaslighting yourself.

The therapist who understands narcissistic abuse will not keep a straight face but will show you empathy. They will be horrified to hear what happened to you and both their words and facial expressions will validate your negative experience.

The healing journey is your journey and it's your job, you will be the one going through it—and it will be difficult. **It is important that you find supportive helpers along the way.** It is eventually better not to have any therapist than to have one who is invalidating you and making it worse with their position of authority. There are therapists out there who will get you, but you might need some time to find them.

Don't hesitate to ask them before you meet to look into the dynamics of narcissistic abuse if they don't know about it. Vet them according to their experience or willingness to understand it. It is your life and you don't owe anything to anyone. *A therapist is there to help you—not to hinder you further.*

Channel Your Negative Experiences Into Gratitude

Gratitude practices are strongly linked to mental health and overall life satisfaction. Grateful people experience more love, joy and enthusiasm and gratitude serves as a shield from destructive emotions like envy, bitterness and greed. It reduces the risk for depression and anxiety, and it can prevent maladaptive behaviours such as substance abuse or addictions. And it's not just a warm and uplifting feeling, it also benefits the body—if you practice gratitude you can cope better with stress, recover more quickly from illnesses and it even have a positive effect on the immune system.

Yet it is incredibly difficult to find things to be grateful for when your life has been wrecked, when you're mentally, emotionally and physically drained, when you lost all hope and someone you had trusted and loved turned out to be your biggest enemy.

I've been there. My dark thoughts and terrible memories were devouring me alive—*there was no happy place inside me to look for an iota of gratitude.*

But it is possible to channel your negative emotions and rewrite your narrative while expressing gratitude.

Not everything happens for a reason and bad things happen to good people—you are living proof of it, if you escaped from the grasp of a narcissist one way or the other. You don't need to look for a silver lining in your dark times. You don't need to be overly positive—how could you be?

But still, the way you look at things shapes your attitude, and while you shouldn't sugarcoat your terrible experiences, you can put them into perspective by reversing the narrative of it.

Here's how to do it:

1. Take a piece of paper and a pen. I find that handwriting connects you better with yourself than typing on a computer or on a phone—but if it's preferable, open a new file on your laptop or phone.

2. Start writing a list about everything negative that happened to you while you were in a relationship with the narcissist.

275

3. Write short sentences describing
- The things that they did
- The ways they hurt you
- The feelings you felt
- The fears that were consuming you
- The good things that they took away

4. Go into details and get a long exhaustive list. Don't worry if it's repetitive, you don't need to show it to anyone or publish it. It can be as messy or structured as you want it to be, depending on your state of mind and the time you want to spend with it. You can easily spend hours just by listening to all the horrible things they did.

5. Reverse the narrative. Change the narrative of the negative things into something that they can no longer do to you or that you no longer need to tolerate. Take back your power.

"They always mocked my clothes." will turn into *"I am grateful that I can wear any clothing I like without getting a negative comment for it. I am grateful that I have my unique style."*

"They kept calling me clingy." will turn into *" I am grateful that I can express my love and appreciation to the people that matter in my life".*

"They never took the trash out." will turn into *"I am grateful that I don't need to rely on them doing a favour for me and I am in control of my own environment."*

The point of the exercise is threefold:

First, you are getting everything out of your system, all the hurt, all the pain, all the humiliation. You are free to express your opinion, you don't need to suppress your emotions, you don't need to walk on eggshells. You can be open about how much they hurt you and you can be honest about the little irritating things that you never dared to bring up to them to avoid the consequential drama.

Second, you make yourself aware that losing some things means that you are gaining other things. You can now have the clarity to see in a list all the things they wronged you with and you can see how much your boundaries were violated.

Third, you can see how life is better without them—with tangible emotional and physical proof.

Do Something
That You Are Really Bad At

When life is really uncertain and you look for some solid ground to stand on, it is easy to lose motivation for things that you are supposed to be good at. When you feel that just getting out of bed is already an accomplishment of the day, it is hard to keep doing the things that you usually do. You have sky-high expectations towards yourself, you are your own worst critic. You can't seem to reach the level that you are used to from yourself, and it just sends you into a downward spiral—you lack motivation, you make yourself do it, you think you suck at it, you feel that you are a failure, hence you are even less motivated to keep at it.

There are times when improvement seems impossible and while you expect to become better, you feel stuck. Your beloved hobby turns into a chore, your lifelong dream seems ridiculous and your previous accomplishments feel unattainable—yet again.

From good to great is the way that you would want to go, *but you feel that you are not even good enough.*

This is when you have to think differently about your own skills. This is when it's good to start something that you are clearly terrible at.

Motivation comes after accomplishment, and when you feel stuck and unmotivated, any kind of accomplishment seems out of reach.

Start something that you are unfamiliar with

Getting from zero to one is not such a big deal. Becoming great at something that you are already good at is a different kind of learning curve. If you start from zero skill, picking up a thing or two, giving yourself the feeling of accomplishment is just the motivation you need.

If you are an already skilled piano player, when you are down and depressed, you won't get significantly better—you only stay on the level you already have. But if you never touched a piano, even a few hours of practice can give you a sense of accomplishment, as you first manage to strike your first keys—no matter how badly.

If you are a runner, running a little faster or better won't cut it if you are down. Your expectations of how quickly you should improve will be killing it for you. However, if you never ran in your life, running for even 2 minutes at a snail's pace will give you a feeling of success, because the accomplishment is visible. Before, you couldn't run at all, and now, you did it!

Choose something useless

When we pick up a new hobby, we already expect something from it.

Maybe you could sell your cross-stitch artwork on Etsy. Maybe you will run a marathon and lose 50 pounds. Maybe you can become a baker if you learn how to bake bread. It's all wonderful, and you definitely should have ambitions.

But when you use a pastime to pull yourself out from a depressed state, you should do something that you don't have any hidden agenda for.

If you decide to learn to play the ukulele, it's kind of useless, it is just for fun and you can't set the bar too high.

Progressive repetition

Have you ever done a repetitive task, even just copy-pasting huge numbers of items from one file to another? When there is a key combination that you realize to be the best and quickest way?

It starts with figuring out the right way of doing it, then repeating it so many times that your movements are automatic. There is great pleasure in repetitive tasks; and funnily enough, they are not the exact same movements at the beginning and in the middle of the process. You seem to repeat the same, but you are actually improving—you use up less space, you are quicker, you are more effective.

With a new skill, you learn bit by bit. You practice the motions and you repeat them. It can be about doing a push-up correctly—or learning to use photoshop to do a basic design task. It seems to be a mindless repetition, but it still needs concentration and focus—if it's a little challenging, it can even get you in a flow state.

According to Wikipedia, in positive psychology, a flow state, also known **colloquially** as being in the zone, is the mental state of operation in which a person performing an activity is fully immersed in a feeling of energised focus, full involvement, and enjoyment in the process of the activity. In essence, flow is characterised by the complete absorption in what one does, and a resulting loss in one's sense of space and time.

The flow state requires two factors:
- You need to have the **ability** and skill to do the task,
- and it needs to be just a little **challenging.**

If you have the skill but it's not challenging, you will get bored. If it's too much of a challenge, you will get frustrated. The flow state is a progressive state where your skills are increasing as you want to meet the challenge. This is how playing the piano—for example—can get you in the flow state easily, as the more skilled you get, you can take on bigger challenges.

The simpler the task is, the bigger the effect of repetition becomes. You don't need to think about it, you just have to do it; and by repeating it, almost mindlessly will get you in a state where thinking is not uselessly overdone.

Don't expect it to become your life, do it for fun

As the little repetitions pile up you will inevitably become better—and compared to being a complete beginner at it, you will see accomplishment quite quickly.

If you start doing push ups, you don't need to think about breaking the world record, it will still occupy your mind, providing you with distraction and feelings of success. If you never knew how to bake a cake, putting your first cake on the table will feel like a huge step. If you looked at the Greek alphabet as if it was a bunch of squiggles on the page, in no time you will be able to read words in Greek if you spend 10 minutes a day studying them. If you never knew how to take a picture with your phone, spend 10 minutes a day looking at free tutorials about photography and compare your first and last image of a month to see how progress is made.

You are allowed to do something just for fun, to not be useful, to not make sense.

Choosing a distraction to make you feel better is a great way to work on your mental health.

Don't Suppress Your Anger

When you think about someone who needs anger management, red face, tense shoulders, clenched jaw, balled fists, yelling and aggression will usually come to mind first. By definition, the goal of anger management is to reduce both your emotional feelings and the physiological arousal that anger causes.

Anger as a feeling is neither good nor bad.

Like every other emotion, it's conveying a message, telling you something about the actual situation and about your relation to it. It's perfectly normal to feel angry when you've been mistreated or wronged. Anger becomes a problem only when you express it in a way that harms yourself or others.

But what if you are over-managing your anger? What if the problem is the exact opposite? What if you are that kind of person, who never gets angry?

What if your reaction to an upsetting situation goes against your very nature and instead of experiencing and managing your anger you are suppressing it so it doesn't harm anyone else—leaving you extremely vulnerable, as it is detrimental both for your mind and body.

When I went to see a sexual therapist to help me overcome some problems—I sat across her, wringing my hands, telling my story about my ex, how we met, how he turned from the love of my life into an abusive monster, how he humiliated me, violated me in more ways than I could talk about. I told her about it all, as focused and short as possible—I didn't want to really talk about it, I wanted to get to the point of the solution, not the problem itself. I knew the problem: it was him. I wanted closure, I wanted someone to tell me that I was wronged, and it was unfair.

But instead, she asked me: *"Are you not angry at him?"*

I was in shock. I *just* told her about my past years of traumatic events, the last one being the victim of revenge porn and she asks me if I am angry. Well, damn, I am. And I told her so.

285

"You talk about it as objectively and casually, as you were telling someone else's story about going grocery shopping. You don't show any emotion, there is no anger in your voice—this is why I am asking, if you are angry at all."

I could feel tears welling up in my eyes and with a trembling soft voice I answered that I am so very angry and disappointed that I could scream and shout, but *I am terrified that if I let myself feel all of it*, my rage will eat me up and it will be like opening a faucet and I have no idea what will come out and if I can ever close it. I told her that I am scared of it, as the amount of rage I have inside could set a full town on fire, and I cannot risk lashing it out on anyone.

I told her I was meditating a lot, practising breathing and that I was considering to take up yoga again.

She looked at me and said:

Well... *fuck yoga, you are already way too zen. You need another approach...*

Emotional avoidance

Emotions have their own lives within our minds. They are there for a reason, to guide us, to stop us, to push us forward. You need to live with your emotions, you need to acknowledge their presence because if they are ignored and suppressed they will find a way to come back, in the form of health issues, mental illness, stress—and it can get out of control very easily.

In my case, I needed anger management, but not as in managing my anger and my outbursts to stop them from getting out of control. I needed to stop suppressing it, finding a healthy outlet and a pace for it to be released on my own terms—so I can learn to live with them, resolve them and move on.

Many of us learned during childhood to ignore or avoid bad things. But this ignoring bad experiences, and how you feel about them will not make things better at all. In fact, the more you put off dealing or even acknowledging that something is wrong, the worse it becomes. Mental health experts refer to this as **"emotional avoidance."**

You need to take the time to learn about healthy ways to deal with your anger, or even how to recognise your feelings in the first place.

Repressed anger tends to have deep roots, going all the way back to childhood, and it can be hard to manage. Creating a safe space for you to process your anger in productive ways can be crucial. It can happen with the help of a therapist, but some practices can be exercised also on your own.

It is important to learn to release the anger; that you release it for yourself in a safe way; and to realize that anger and violence are not the same things. A healthy release of anger never involves abuse or violence of yourself or another or any living being.

Sadly, the occurrences are still prevalent in our society.

There are active and passive actions to manage repressed anger.

Fighting repressed anger actively

The active part is finding ways to open Pandora's box at your own pace, on your own terms—consciously choosing your actions. These are not the same methods that anger management and therapy would suggest, anger management here means to help to bring that anger up to the surface.

Channel your anger into physical activity

#1 Punch a pillow

As childish as it might sound, it is a simple and easy way to use physical activity as an outlet to your anger. Carve out some time for yourself, and start punching a pillow, reminding yourself of your own anger, bringing it back up on the surface. Think about how you were wronged, how you felt, how helpless it made you—and watch how the pace and strength of your punches increase. Keep at it for long enough—if need be, set a timer, for at least 5–10 minutes. The exercise starts with feeling a little puzzled about it, not really getting the hang of it first, but as time passes it becomes more powerful, and you know you're done when your feelings fade, and you don't feel the need to punch anymore. Repeat it daily, for 5–10 minutes and notice how you feel afterwards.

#2 Start a violent sport

My sport of choice was kickboxing. It is physically taxing and requires a lot of focus and stamina. Besides the general advantages of the sport, the focused punching and kicking of a punching bag is an excellent way to manage anger in a controlled way. Initially, I needed to picture my ex onto the bag, kicking and punching his imaginary self in front of me. The mental image I had helped me to exert such a force I didn't even know I had in me. With the careful instructions of my coach, I managed to develop also a technique for both the kicks and punches. It gave an ecstatic thrill of an adrenaline rush, all my emotions washing over me, my body and mind screaming for a break, but I was on a mission— to let it all out.

Any type of martial art is brilliant to coordinate the body and mind, increase stamina and give back a sense of previously unknown power. Not to mention the fact that it fights your internal feeling of helplessness and lack of power, just by physically getting stronger, knowing that you could defend yourself.

I am at a point where I would advise *anyone* against attacking me on a street or anywhere else. And it is not about being violent, it is being powerful enough not to be afraid anymore.

#3 Shout it from the rooftops

Another great practice is the controlled shouting, which is in reality as simple as it sounds. If you are as reserved and composed as I am, you are not going to be used to shouting—except if you are a sports fan where you can cheer loudly for your team. There are therapy sessions that involve a hike into deserted areas, forests, rivers, out of the city—but this can be done just as well on your own. The deserted area is necessary not to hold you back, not to let your inhibitions stop you.

All you need to do is shout and scream, focus on what bothers you, now you can do it, watch how your emotions start bubbling up and start screaming and shouting. Keep at it as long as it feels good and let go of any feelings of it being silly or useless. Just shout, let it all out. If you feel awkward about it, take music with you, put on your headphones and set the music to the loudest volume—and let it out.

#4 Sing your heart out

This works on the same principle as shouting. Singing, in general, has multiple beneficial effects on you. Singing helps in releasing endorphins and oxytocin. It is known to decrease stress and anxiety. Both of these hormones can make you feel better in general and decrease any pain you might be feeling. Singing can also lower your blood pressure, cause you to have lower cortisol levels, and decrease your stress and anxiety, it will certainly have a positive effect on your immune system.

If you use it as an outlet for your repressed anger the additional benefits will be a calmer, more relaxed, less stressed you. The good thing is that even singing in the car or in the shower can have a great effect—and it surely will improve your mood.

Dealing with the already surfaced emotion

The passive way is to restore the balance, once the anger is already back on the surface, where you can already deal with it. These practices are most common and well-known, and they can help in balancing any type of negative emotion—not just anger, but anxiety, stress and even overthinking.

As there is a lot to read about them, I am just offering a quick summary of the most common ones:

#1 Mindfulness and meditation

Simple relaxation tools, such as deep breathing and relaxing imagery, can help calm down disturbed feelings. There are books and courses that can teach you relaxation techniques, and once you learn the techniques, you can call upon them in any situation. But just focusing and being present, practising mindfulness is a great way to get grounded in your present. Focus on the present, notice the positive things no matter how small they are. Celebrate your small wins, reward yourself whenever you can. *You can't overdo self-care.*

#2 Calming physical activities

Choose some calming activities that can soothe your mind—and keep at it, best to make a habit of pursuing them. It can be yoga, walking, jogging, running, stretching, pilates—whatever rocks your boat.

The obvious benefits of physical activity of your choice are improved strength and stamina, reduced stress and anxiety levels, a decrease in a multitude of health risks, such as cardiovascular diseases, improved sleep quality, better cognitive functioning, and also the forming of better eating habits.

#3 Crying as a mindful practice

Crying is a natural response humans have to a range of emotions, including sadness, grief, joy, and frustration. Among other benefits, crying has a soothing effect, it helps to relieve pain by releasing oxytocin and endorphins. It alleviates both mental and physical pain; with the help of the two hormones. Crying reduces stress and it can help you to sleep better.

Anger is just an emotion. It's not good or bad. It guides you, it shows you that something is off. Dealing with anger, on the other hand, is a **conscious choice**—and it should be managed in a way that it doesn't harm either you or others. If you are the kind of person who has trouble expressing anger and rather suppresses it, your kind of anger management will consist of different elements from someone's who cannot control their temper.

You need to learn to allow your anger to surface, by actively looking for methods to let it out in a controlled way, so that you can deal with it and process it. Being zen is admirable, but sometimes it is not what you need. To know what your body and mind needs *is mindfulness*, but it can and should take different forms. **Sometimes punching and kicking is just exactly the kind of mindful zen that you need.**

How Writing Helps You Heal

I have always been writing, as a way of self-expression, as a hobby, as therapy. I always kept a journal. I was blogging. I wrote poems and short stories. It was my go-to method to deal with life—even before I knew I subconsciously used it as therapy.

When I came out from my abusive relationship, after the initial numbness and shock, my emotions were overflowing and I couldn't possibly process them. I went to therapy, but it was just 50 minutes a week. I talked to my mom and a friend of mine, but I couldn't burden them with my circular and repetitive thoughts over and over again. My mind was spinning in circles and there was no outlet, but the paper to try and make sense of the tsunami of emotions and hurt inside me.

On top of it, I had a lot of free time. I didn't realize it but being with a narcissist was a 24/7 job and I was revolving around him all the time. Now that he was gone, I had too much time and too few ideas what to do with it. I didn't know about self-care because this wasn't how I was conditioned. I was used to taking care of my ex.

So I had to pick up new things to do and writing was a good way to start. I was journaling. I wrote down my feelings, sometimes it was coherent, others it was just ramblings and whining page after page. I was writing poems, trying to put some beauty in the terror I felt.

I was writing articles trying to collect information that I thought others would find useful. The sense of helping others was giving me purpose.

Freewriting and journaling were great ways, but the best way for me was to write with the expectation of publishing it—for the whole world to see it.

Writing organizes your thoughts

Life happens and it happens quickly. When it does you can't stop to contemplate your decisions and process your feelings, you just go with the flow, you put one foot after the other and you move on. Adrenaline keeps you going, stress helps you survive. *Until the storm passes you weather it.*

But then? Then you need to deal with all the emotions bottled up. You need to see it and make sense of it. You need to organize your thoughts. You arrange them into chunks and try to make them fit into a system. You have a point to deliver. You have something to say. Arranging your thoughts and feelings into an article, tidying them up and clearing the fog, making the messages comprehensible. Sometimes these messages come to you, the information passed on to others, you too will get it, finally. Writing helps you find a structured and clear way to express what has been inside your mind without recognising its proper value. Trying to get the message to others forces you to arrange it into a comprehensive system that will allow you to understand it easier too.

Writing gives you a new perspective

When you are living your life and the days are passing by, sometimes you stop, wonder and begin looking at things from a different perspective. When the amount of events is overwhelmingly high and out of proportion, this mindfulness, and conscious perspective-shifting become impossible. You are dragged forward to the next day and the next after. And you are stuck in your own perspective for what seems like forever. Maybe there is nothing wrong with your perspective, but more often than not it is distorted by your beliefs and expectations.

Writing it down offers a fresh perspective and new beginnings. You can become objective about things that were tormenting you, you can be rationally looking for the reasons after so many years of not finding any.

Writing helps to process your story, to tweak the narrative and add some learnings and conclusions

Writing about my trauma makes me vulnerable.

I open up and basically invite strangers to judge me, hurt and scrutinize me. And sometimes they treat you in a way that really leaves scars behind, and it hurts. But the risk of being hurt is so much lower than all the benefits of making sense of the trauma.

When you finally understand, when the puzzle pieces fit, when you realize where you made a mistake, where you should have made a different decision, it is often a turning point. When you finally forgive yourself, knowing you did everything and nothing could have changed the past, when you stop trying to understand the incomprehensible but you accept and you are able to move on, writing makes trauma tolerable, as it gives meaning to it, it enacts forgiveness, it reflects your evolution instead of looking for someone else to blame.

Writing allows you to feel

Suppressing emotions is a dangerous thing. Not finding a way to release your anger, your fear, your hatred—it might depict you as someone who has their act together, but more likely it will have mental and medical side effects.

In an abusive relationship, people start to lose their relation to reality, and they lose their ways. For mere survival, you start to suppress certain feelings at first. You suppress your fear, your anger, your frustration. It doesn't help you, so it has to go.

Writing about your feelings, giving power to your words will allow you to feel those feelings, to allow yourself the luxury of being angry—without lashing out at anyone.

Writing about trauma helps others not to feel alone

We all think that our traumas are unique, we are afraid we will be judged, we are ashamed that it happened to us. Until it turns out that many people can relate to our pain. Until we learn that many feel relieved that it didn't just happen to them. Until our words make people belong and understand.

The worst thing about trauma is that it isolates you, it shuts you off from your connections. You hide and you lie about it-because talking about it is hard and there is no guarantee that talking will help, so you expose yourself for no reason. I had more than one experience with trusting friends with my problems who shrugged it away, joked about it or made me feel so awkward, that I had to apologise for being abused.

With writing, you are coming out on your own terms and your readers react on theirs. If you touch someone with your story, they will let you know. If they are bored or feeling awkward, they can simply stop reading. No discussion is needed.

It's therapy at your own pace

You can do it as often or as rarely as it feels right. If it is every day—you are allowed. If you are writing about one single event in multiple pieces, trying to figure out even more—you can do that. If you feel better after it—it's good. If you feel worse—it can mean that it is deeper than you thought and it might suggest that you should seek external help, as in speaking to a therapist. Otherwise, feeling worse after writing could mean that you are finally opening yourself to the trauma and its effects on you.

There is no deadline, there is no rush. You can do it from anywhere. You can do it anytime. It's yours and yours only—independent from external circumstances. Writing can be your safe haven where you are allowed to feel and think at your own pace.

7. CLOSING THE BOX FULL OF DARKNESS

Never Again:
Recognising The First Signs

When you are out of the relationship, you know that you are better off. And you also know that you need to be more careful next time. Because *there will be a next time.* You will heal and you will thrive. You will date again, and you will fall in love again.

But you will strive to never allow anyone to hurt you—ever again.

You know what it feels like. You know how easy it was to manipulate you, because you didn't know what to watch out for. Now you will recognise all the red flags better. You will pay attention to the yellow flags as well, even though they don't yet signal imminent danger, but you know better than to turn your head to something that is seemingly innocent but suspicious.

You won't need to get paranoid. You won't need to shut everyone out. **But you will watch out better for emotional predators.**

If you meet someone decent, no matter how hard you look, they won't raise red flags. If someone's values match yours, then you won't have to ever question them. If someone knows how to respect boundaries without even knowing yours—just out of common human decency they are respectful in maintaining general boundaries—then they won't push them deliberately or inadvertently.

Watching out for red flags is a necessary survival tool for those who have at least once needed to survive abusive relationships.

What does *'watch out for red flags'* really mean and what it doesn't.

It Doesn't Mean You're Paranoid

Being paranoid means that you see danger where there is none. The current world is full of emotional predators and they are especially prevalent in online dating. Watching out for possible harm means that you are cautious, not paranoid.

It Doesn't Mean You're Overreacting

You are not hysterical; you are not overreacting. You see the situations as they are and you respond to them keeping your own safety and well-being in mind.

It Doesn't Mean You Don't Trust Anyone

Just because someone destroyed the trust you built together it doesn't mean that everyone else will. You are still capable of trust, but you tread lightly when giving people chances—especially second chances.

It Doesn't Mean You Stay Away From Everyone

Watching out for red flags doesn't mean that you stay away from people. The contrary. It means that you are seeking company, but you are choosing carefully who to spend your precious time with.

It Means That You Know Your Boundaries

If you suffered first-hand from an emotional predator, then now you know your boundaries. If you never had a bad experience, it means that you learnt from others' mistakes. Taking care of yourself means that you respect your own boundaries and demand others to respect them too.

It Means That You're Aware of Potential Harm

Knowing what can hurt you and what is harmless is a fine line—especially these days when the first abusive signs can be so subtle. If you've educated yourself about potential harm, it means that you will recognise toxic behaviour and you can act accordingly, prioritising your own well-being.

It Means That You Expect Decent Behaviour

With suffering comes maturity. Maybe a kind of maturity that you never wanted, but you still have it. Now you know what to expect from others, you recognise the behaviour that you expect and also what you don't tolerate. It's not having expectations that are too high. It's having the right kind of them.

It Means That You Can Say No

Watching out for red flags means that when you see them you can say no. Your previous experience taught you that saying no is not selfish, it's necessary. And as you paid a high price for this lesson, *you cherish your ability to say no to whatever doesn't feel right.*

It Means That You Trust Your Instincts

Intuition. Gut feeling. Hunch. Feeling off about something. They are signals from our brain to be careful. Your instincts are there for a very good reason—they keep you safe and out of harm's way. If you watch out for red flags it means that you trust your ability to size up a situation and move away if it doesn't feel good. It's not some hocus-pocus, it's based on evidence from your past that taught you a lesson. All you have to do is to be tuned in with yourself and never question your judgment.

If you ever see a red flag, you will know and feel that you need to be careful. You can still be open-minded; you can still be curious—but you have learned that *self-care is not selfish*. And I repeat, watching out for red flags will not create them. Toxic behaviour creates them—and that's what you need to avoid.

Too Good to Be True

The narcissists don't know boundaries and they don't know the concept of doing things in moderation. If they do something, they are all in, or they just don't do it. This is how they love-bomb you to the extent of larger-than-life-kind-of-love. This is how they stonewall you—taking everything away. This is how they discard you—overnight without looking back. Until they come back with the force of a hurricane to hoover you back into their world.

They do everything to an extreme.

And now that you know them, you can also see how they have exaggerated even on a first date. So, when you start dating again, these are the exaggerations to watch out for:

Too Honest

Honesty, transparency, integrity, kindness. They are great character traits, and this is exactly what we are all looking for in a partner. We would like to build a relationship with someone we can trust, someone who won't manipulate us, who will act as they speak and who behaves decently.

Toxic individuals will explicitly emphasize values they do not have to make you think of them in a positive light. They are the ones who will explicitly say that they are "really nice guys", that they would "never lie to you", that they "value transparency and integrity more than anything." If you realize that your date talks about grandiose words when describing themselves, beware!

A genuinely honest and transparent individual won't feel the urge to advertise themselves excessively and they don't need to shed a much better light on them to make a good impression.

Too Much Information

Toxic individuals have a tendency to speed up the dating process—for they want to reel you in quickly, to secure your emotions that they can feed off. It means showing early signs of affection. It means too much information in a really short time. It means an almost interrogation kind of conversation to get to know you better. If you find yourself on a first date where suddenly you learn everything about your date, from their childhood, through their traumas to their latest accomplishments, watch out.

Dating should be slow progress. I'm not talking about waiting until the third date before sleeping with someone, I am talking about the natural way of conversation.

It's great to get to know your date, but at the first date you don't need to become privy to everything they have ever done, and they don't need to learn everything about you either.

If the oversharing raises a red flag, even if you can't really put a finger on it—trust your instincts, for they are there for a reason. If it feels too quick or off, then chances that it could develop into something unhealthy.

Too Much Attention

We all want attention. We all want to be wanted. We all want to feel that our date is interested. But it has to be practised in moderation—just as everything. On a first date, it is crucial to feel that our date is interested, and they want to keep up the conversation just as much as we do. With a toxic individual, you can be subjected to an excessive amount of flattery, praise and overall too much attention.

If you find yourself in the crossfires of an interrogative attitude about your feelings, childhood, friends, favourite foods—watch out. These things are great to discover over time, but it doesn't need to happen within the first thirty minutes.

Also, in case they are already planning to introduce you to their family, friends and planning their holidays with you or hinting that they could settle down with you and finally have kids—be very alert. This is called *future-faking*, and it's a very common toxic tactic.

They are master manipulators and exquisite conversationalists, who always know what to say and how to say it.

Too Many Exes And Fans

They say you should never talk about exes on a first date, but in reality, our exes are part of our lives. They shaped us and made us into who we are now, so it's only natural to drop a few hints about learnings or likes and dislikes.

But you shouldn't list all your exes and they shouldn't take over the whole conversation throughout the date.

If you notice that your date is talking way too much of their exes and it seems they had a full harem of them that they boast about, it's another red flag. Usually, they talk about the exes with a negative tone too, always concluding that you are definitely better than them. Don't trust someone who is giving you more credit after 30 minutes than to someone they have spent a significantly longer amount of time. You might be better than them, but they have no way of knowing about it, so it is just a triangulation tactic to reel you in. Beware.

Also, having way too many people they rely on for external validation can be a sign of unhealthy attachment styles or an unusual need for admiration and external validation.

Too Much Flirting

They say that you can judge someone's character from how they are treating the waiter. And it is true on many levels—you can see how they treat someone who is below them, how they treat money, how generous or tight they are with money. But another thing to watch out for is if they get extremely flirty with the waitress or waiter, or the bartender, barista etc.

If someone has a compulsive need to get even more attention than you are giving them that's a sign for their mask slipping.

They love the attention, they adore the spotlight and they will do anything to get some extra eyes on them, wherever they go. You might find it charming that they are easy going to the point of chatting with the couple sitting at the next table, but if you notice a pattern of trying to get everyone's attention, it's not a good sign.

Most importantly: trust your instincts! Your gut feelings are valid, and you don't need to apologise for them or explain them to anyone, not even to yourself.

If you feel something off, slow down, take a step back and look out for yourself unapologetically. You are your own responsibility and a decent person won't corner you into something where you feel uncomfortable.

Not Everything Happens
For a Reason

When I started to heal after my abusive relationship, I spent months trying to figure out the reasons. I was trying to find some sense in the inexplicable. I spent a long time torturing myself by looking for answers for questions that shouldn't have been even there to ask.

It was horrible. And at the same time, it was necessary. I was trying what my brain wanted the most: to find meaning where there was none, to cater to the oh-so-natural human need of cognitively grasping the world.

It took me a long time to realize that my quest for learning about all the reasons was not taking me anywhere. Because there were no right answers to impossible questions. After all, how could you make sense of something nonsensical? How could you find a reasonable explanation for the unnecessary and meaningless hurt that came from the very person who was supposed to love you?

It was a dark time. The darkest of all.

But eventually, I came to realize that the questions I am asking have nothing to do with my future life. They were questions about a past that shouldn't have happened and they were questions that weren't supposed to provide me with any closure.

The right questions came only after I let go of the idea of finding meaning.

There is a popular concept that 'everything happens for a reason.' And as much as it tries to be comforting, it is infuriating. When we say that the inexplicable happens according to a master plan that we don't see or understand, we are cognitively surrendering to the unknown, and it is supposed to give us peace of mind. It gives us a pseudo-closure and it takes away our responsibility. But it also renders us purposeless in a wicked game, where we don't have a say.

If things—bad things—can happen for a reason that we are not privy to, it strips us from our ability to decide about our own lives and suggests that fatalism is the only way to go. It takes away our agency, as we couldn't have had any means of changing the course of events then, so how could we now?

In fairness, if I look back on it, I could have prevented the abuse. There was a time when I knew what was going on and I could have left then. I had a choice, I really did. But I stayed. *I ignored the red flags.* I surrendered to my feelings instead of making rational decisions. I chose not to see what I should have seen. Because there were things that clouded my judgment more than I care to admit. I did make a bad decision, but I still believe that there was no real reason. It was unnecessary and meaningless.

All I had to do was to let go of trying to understand… But this is not how we are wired. We are wired to understand and understanding comes after letting go of this eternal quest for answers.

One of my favourite quotes is:

> *"We cannot change the inevitable. The only thing we can do is play on the one string we have, and that is our attitude. I am convinced that life is 10% what happens to me and 90% of how I react to it."* — CHARLES R SWINDOLL

This quote doesn't speak about the reason. It doesn't speak about blame. It doesn't speak about growing. All it says is that **we have the power of rewriting our own narrative** and whatever we perceive good or bad will be determined not by the events, but our own mindset.

When I finally let go of trying to find the explanation, there came a time that was a lot more fruitful and it offered me more closure than any made-up reason could ever have. I realized that I can choose how I look at my trauma. I realized that it is up to me to decide if I let it define me or not.

It didn't have universal learning attached to it. It wasn't that I needed to know my boundaries better or to become better at recognizing toxic people, no. The learning was that this life is made up of events that have the power to shape us—*but only to the extent that we will allow them.*

When I let go of wanting to explain why it happened, I finally had the clarity to shift the perspective into what I can take out of it—even if it was terrible. Especially because it was terrible.

The internet is full of fake positivity and helpful advice. But it is a trap. When you are really low, faking positivity is a trap. You cannot fake positivity until you feel positive, not after you were raped, assaulted or abused; not after losing a loved one in an inexplicable and cruel way; not after losing a child (which is the biggest of horrors) that can ever happen to anyone.

You don't need to be positive about any of it. These events are not to spark positivity.

But you need to admit what they can teach you and you can choose to look at the learnings in a positive way-even if you didn't ask for any of it. Of course, you didn't ask for it. Of course, you didn't deserve it. But you were handed this, and now it's your time to decide what you will do about it and how you will incorporate the learnings into your future.

My abuser was mean. He was unnecessarily cruel. He hurt me just because he could. There was not one single reason for him raping me and beating me and leaving me with a one-year-old baby-other than because this is what he chose to do. According to a decent mind, there are no explanations for this.

I learnt a lesson that I never asked for. I learnt it, because there was nothing else to do but learn it and accept it.
It changed me.

And this change—whether I wanted it or not, whether I needed it or not-was the mandatory outcome that I needed to incorporate in my life. I was given this change and there was nothing to do about it, but to accept it and learn from it. As when I tried to fight it and I resisted it, it didn't go anywhere.

Our biggest teachers in life are the most unexpected ones. It is possible that you learnt a lot from your parents and from your partners. It is possible that your kids teach you, or your colleagues teach you lessons that slowly shape you, making you a different person. But we are all conditioned by our learnings and experiences.

An abusive event, a loss of a loved one, a mental health problem—they are going to be your biggest teachers, whether you like it or not. And the only thing that is sensible to do is to embrace the change they are forcing you through. My biggest learning, after the abuse, was that there are times when I need to stop fighting the inevitable. The inevitable wasn't the rape-that could have been avoided, for example by him deciding not to do it-it was the change in me.

How Can You Embrace That You Changed and Make the Most Of it?

Acknowledge that you changed. Stop fighting it, stop trying to go back to where you were, because these events leave an indelible mark on you whether you want it, or like it or not.

Spot the differences and look for the positive change in character. How did you change? Did you get better at judging people? Did you get more introverted? Did you get stronger? Did you gain a certain clarity about people and life in general?

Embrace the positive change. Applaud yourself for everything that you have learned—disregard the circumstances of it entirely. If it wasn't for the trigger, but you got more resilient, isn't that a good thing? Strip the negative events of the positive change and focus on the change itself.

Stop looking backward. Stop saying things like *"I am only strong because I have to be."* <u>No, you are strong because you choose to be strong</u>. You could break down; you could be weak—yet you are not. You are strong and you are doing better than ever.

Use your acquired strengths for something new. Make something good out of the things leading to changing you. Do you have a better understanding of people now that you have been hurt? Great! Use it! Go out and meet some new people, armed with your invisible knowledge and congratulate yourself every step along the way when you use your newly found understanding.

Let go of the idea that everything happens for a reason. The world isn't created to cater to our needs and there are things that have absolutely no reason. Stop looking for something that might not exist. Instead, focus your attention on things you can have an impact on, such as your well-being, self-care and helping others.

7 Life-Changing Truths After Abuse

Healing is tough because through the process we open up our wounds and let them bleed again so they can be closed and healed once and for all. Abuse shapes us, but it doesn't have to define us. To be able to make room for the experiences we need to understand a few things about it. That being said, below are 7 life-changing truths that can serve as affirmations to help you reclaim your power.

1. It's Never Been Your Fault

No matter what your abuser, society or the legal system tells you about your involvement: **abuse is never the fault of the victim**. We are all adults and as such we have the capability to make informed and conscious decisions. If someone abuses you, it's their decision—and no matter what you did, how much alcohol you consumed or what you wore, it's not your fault.

The blame belongs exclusively to the abuser. No one has the right to take advantage of you by their own decision. *Don't buy into victim-blaming, it's not your fault. It never was.*

2. You Didn't Deserve It

Abuse is not transactional. No matter what you did, you didn't deserve it. No act from your side could be an excuse or an explanation for any form of abuse. If someone assaulted you, it has nothing to do with you and everything to do with them.

You didn't ask for it. It's easy to shift the blame by saying it takes two to tango or that you shouldn't have stayed, you should have left, you should have defended yourself or drawn clearer boundaries. **Abuse is not a punishment for anything you do— it's a crime to be punished on its own.**

3. It Didn't Damage You Forever

You might think and you could have heard that you are damaged goods. It's true that you have to carry such a heavy emotional burden that it can hold you back and weigh you down, but you're not damaged forever.

In the darkest moments, it's easy to believe that you're hurt so much that it seems impossible to ever become whole again, but the human mind is so exceptional. You won't stay damaged forever.

You may suffer for a long time from its effects, such as PTSD, depression or anxiety. You might even carry the damage with you for longer than you'd like to, but you're not stigmatized, and you're not broken for good.

4. You Can, and You Will Heal

I've been there. I know how it feels. As if there would never again be anything to feel happy about. As if the darkness that they dragged you into, would consume you whole. It looks desperate and it feels too overwhelming to ever process.

But you can and will heal. There is life after abuse, even if it feels impossible to get out of the haze. You have choices and you can get your agency back. You have to lean on your support network, seek the company of those you trust, you need to get away from your abuser—and you will heal.

The learnings that you get from the abuse will make you stronger, you will learn how to engage in better self-care, how to have better relationships, how to ask for your wants and needs. You can learn to express yourself better and you will recognise the red flags easier.

5. You Are Not Crazy

Healing starts with acknowledging abuse. You need to learn to trust yourself again, for you might have been gaslighted into thinking that you deserved it, that it wasn't that bad, that it's you who is abusive or that you are lying.

Your instincts and feelings are valid. Don't let anyone invalidate them just because doing so serves their agenda.

Recognising the abuse, the lack of consent, the trauma, is the first step towards getting back your agency. You need to surround yourself with people who you can trust, whom you believe, who believe in you.

6. You Don't Have to Forgive Your Abuser

They say that to be able to heal, you need to forgive your abuser, for you shouldn't carry hatred or any negative feeling towards them. This is entirely optional and it's your choice. You don't have to forgive your abuser to get closure, you don't need to be the bigger person, you don't need to come up with explanations for their behaviour. You are your only responsibility and you need to take care of only yourself. Your abuser's needs and feelings are not yours to care about.

If you feel better by forgiving them, do it. But it's not a necessity for the healing process. There are crimes that are impossible to forgive, and you shouldn't put another emotional burden on yourself by expecting forgiveness from yourself for the unforgivable.

7. You Deserve Better

No matter what your abuser made you believe by their words or actions, you deserve a healthy, respectful and loving relationship, where your consent, your agency, your sexuality is not endangered. Everyone deserves to be around people who respect them and keep their best interests in mind.

Don't let your abusive experiences define what you think of a relationship. There are people out there, who are not better or more than you, who are cherished, loved and appreciated. And you deserve that—without conditions, without changing, without becoming better in any sense.

To suffer any kind of trauma can be life-changing—but don't let it be life-changing for the worse. Take it as a learning experience. Yes, you have seen the darkness from close-up, but you can get out of it and live a full life again. You can learn, you can heal, you can become stronger.

You learn how to draw your boundaries, how to better stay away from people who don't respect you. Use the power you gained to lift others up, to help others heal by telling your story. You shouldn't ever be invalidated or silenced.

Closing the Box Full of Darkness

A thank-you note

Someone I loved once gave me
a box full of darkness.
It took me years to understand
that this too, was a gift.

—MARY OLIVER

He shattered me, yet I picked up the pieces and put myself back together, laced with gold—like kintsugi. And I want to thank him for that.

Because with everything he has committed against me through the years of verbal, physical and sexual abuse, I have become the woman I was always meant to be. This woman I am now. After I hurt and healed, after I reclaimed myself, bargained it back from all the darkness that wanted to consume me. Because the woman I am now has nothing to do with the one he once knew. That one is just a vague memory, a shadow self of the current me.

And I want to thank him for that.

Had it not been for him I would have never discovered the bottomless well of power and agency within me. The strength and the grit and the ever-liberating, incredible wholesomeness that connects me to the rest of the world. The woman who he chose to abuse, hurt and humiliate in every possible way, is gone, and it now feels she has never been here.

I am stronger

I had been strong before him, but not this strong. He never knew *this* strong. I am stronger because I had no choice but to endure the pain, to live through my days and thrive, to survive and make the best of my life. This strength comes from all the tears I shed, all the sleepless nights, all the falls and bruises that I had to stand up from. It is the independence and the certainty of survival. The circular sureness of being able to do it because I have done it before.

I know my worth

I used to rely on his approval and appreciation to measure my own worth. I used to think that his opinion mattered more than my own. I thought if I became kinder, more attentive, better and simply 'more' then I will earn his acknowledgement.

Of my beauty, my femininity, my life choices. I didn't understand that my worth was not dependent on him, or on anyone. Now I get it. Finally. It took me long enough, but I do. I am me, unapologetically and authentically me: sometimes boring, sometimes clingy, sometimes hurt, sometimes everything you have ever dreamt of—the good, the bad, the ugly and beautiful me. I am lovable and precious whether anyone notices or appreciates my individuality.

I learned to say no

I learned to say no to everyone and everything that doesn't treat me right from the get-go. Be it professional or personal, love, friends or family. I am not afraid of burning bridges and cutting ties. I understand that this time and space and life is my only chance to get things done, to get it right, to be happy. This is my sole responsibility. So, I am saying no to whatever doesn't feel right and I'm learning to say yes to everything that has the opportunity to make me bigger, better, more complete. And if it is risky and uncertain, I will still go with my instincts, following my intuition to lead me to learnings, love or lust.

I listen to my instincts

My instincts are there for a very good reason. Evolutionarily I am wired to fun-seeking and risk-avoiding. Now I am connected to myself more than ever, I feel I have a connection to others, to the wholeness of the universe. And my gut feeling tells me, and it always had, which path to follow, which to abandon. I only need to listen. And trust myself enough to know that I am capable of choosing wisely and carefully. I know enough to trust the process and to not confuse the bend on the road with the end of the road.

I look for things that make me happy and whole

I learnt to look out for myself more than for anyone else. *No one can care more about me than I should.* We all have lives to live, problems to solve, money to make, fun to have. How could we expect anyone else to care for our happiness and wellbeing more than ourselves? We can't. We shouldn't. We are human. We fail. We fail ourselves and we fail others. I learnt the hard way that practising empathy, love and caring for others, while suppressing my own needs will not take us anywhere. Neither of us; as individuals and society. I am responsible for my own life, my own mental health, my own happiness. It cannot depend on anyone else; it cannot come from anyone. I am to be self-sufficient in being the source of my own joy. And so is everyone else. You cannot do the job for someone else; you cannot save someone who refuses to be saved. It's not your job.

I look for real connections

Being over the drama and heartbreak only to realize that the love I had wasn't even real from his side was the most bitter pill to swallow. Learning that what I thought to be the love of my life was a carefully orchestrated string of manipulation tactics… it broke my heart. But I learnt to look for real connections with people who care about me just as much as I care about them. Who will make time for me, who will make just as much of an effort as I am willing to. Who I can connect with on different levels, be it sexual, emotional, intellectual or spiritual. The level doesn't matter. The realness of the connection does. And I refuse to settle for less.

I am unapologetically me

When I was with him, I always wanted to be someone else. Someone prettier, someone better, someone more. And I didn't manage. And I was apologising for things that weren't even mistakes. Now I don't want to be someone else. I want to improve myself, to become an even better version of myself. I am open enough to apologise if I make a mistake or if I hurt someone unintentionally. But I stopped apologising for who I am. Here I am. This is me. This is as good as it gets for the time being… until I know better. *And I have learnt to be unapologetically me,* with all my flaws and imperfections, with my silly perks, with my approach to life. Take it or leave it. I don't reject change but if I change, I'll do it for me, not for anyone else.

I am more and better than I have ever been, and ironically, I have to thank my abuser for this. I grew because of him and despite him.

He gave me a gift. Because I loved him once and the box full of darkness that he gave me was indeed a gift. But I am ready to close it and put it away.

THE END

References

[1] American Psychiatric Association: Diagnostic and Statistical Manual of Mental Disorders: Diagnostic and Statistical Manual of Mental Disorders, Fifth Edition. Arlington, VA: American Psychiatric Association, 2013.

[2] Elsa Ronningstam, PhD 2016, New Insights Into Narcissistic Personality Disorder, Psychiatric Times, Special Reports, retrieved 25 April 2020 <https://www.psychiatrictimes.com/special-reports/new-insights-narcissistic-personality-disorder>

[3] Torgersen, Svenn; Lygren, Sissel; Øien, Per Anders; Skre, Ingunn; Onstad, Sidsel; Edvardsen, Jack; Tambs, Kristian; Kringlen, Einar (December 2000). "A Twin Study of Personality Disorders" <https://www.sciencedirect.com/journal/comprehensive-psychiatry>

[4] Glen O. Gabbard, Gabbard's Treatments Of Psychiatric Disorders, PsychiatryOnline, APA, retrieved 25 April 2020, <https://doi.org/10.1176/appi.books.9781585625048>

[5] Traci Pedersen 2018, Narcissists' Lack of Empathy Tied to Less Gray Matter, PsychCentral, retrieved 25 April 2020 <https://psychcentral.com/news/2013/07/06/narcissists-lack-of-empathy-tied-to-less-gray-matter/56907.html>

[6] Joseph M. Carver, Ph.D., Love and Stockholm Syndrome, viewed 25th April 2020 <https://drjoecarver.makeswebsites.com/clients/49355/File/love_and_stockholm_syndrome.html>

[7] Helen Fisher 2016, Love Is Like Cocaine, Nautilus, viewed 25 April 2020, <http://nautil.us/issue/33/attraction/love-is-like-cocaine>

[8] Williams, K. D.; Sommer, K. L. (1997). "Social ostracism by one's coworkers: Does rejection lead to loafing or compensation?". Personality and Social Psychology Bulletin. 23 (7): 693–706. <doi:10.1177/0146167297237003>

[9] reference to the Wizard of Oz, where the Wicked Witch of the West is using flying monkeys to attack Dorothy and her company

[10] 50 Obstacles to Leaving, 2013, National Domestic Violence Hotline, retrieved 28th April 2020, <https://www.thehotline.org/2013/06/10/50-obstacles-to-leaving-1-10/>

[11] Jessica Eaton 2018, Victim blaming: Is it a woman's responsibility to stay safe?, BBC News, retrieved 28th April 2020, <https://www.bbc.com/news/uk-england-45809169>

[12] https://www.nsvrc.org/statistics

[13] National Crime Victimization Survey (NCVS) 2017, RAINN, retrieved 28th April 2020, <https://www.rainn.org/statistics/criminal-justice-system>

Acknowledgment

This book is a dream come true and proof that nightmares end. It started as a healing journey: messy, confused and frustrated and it required helping hands to mould it into a structured, useful piece.

The biggest thank you goes to my amazing mom whose unconditional, never-ending love was sometimes the only thing to keep me sane. She always believed in me even when I was at my darkest and her fierce love and continuous support made me get through the most difficult times in my life. My mom is my biggest fan and I can never repay her for all the attention and care that she has given to me. Love you!

To my three incredible daughters who believe that I am the best, even when I order pizza for dinner and let them have unlimited screen time so that I could write. You are brilliant, smart, amazing human beings and I am honoured and proud to be your mother. I hope you will be proud of me too.

To my talented brother, Greg, who stood by me with his no-bullshit attitude and who designed the perfect cover for this book even if my nephews were vying for his attention.

To my brilliant editor, Anna Rozwadowska, who gently but strictly helped me get everything in order to turn the messy manuscript into a comprehensive book.

To my writer friends who gave me invaluable advice to make me a better writer all along. Special thanks to Todd Brison for helping me navigate the muddy waters of self-publishing; and Michael Thompson, Nik Göke, Matt Sandrini, Adrian Drew, Brian Pennie, Danny Forest, Ayodeji Awosika, Jordan Gross, Nico Ryan and Zulie Rane for your relentless support and positivity. You have been an inspiration and you never cease to amaze me.

To my friends, Anna, Edina, Gil, Dan, Ariadne, Kyrie, Leonor, Amardeep and Fanni; you believed I could until I believed you and I did. Thank you for standing by me and listening to whatever I had to say. No matter how far you might be, we're still close.

To my kickboxing coach, Arnold, for showing me how to heal and find strength and power through the means of sports and for helping me find peace and mindfulness through punches and kicks. Thank you for believing in me and showing me how badass I can be.

And to all my readers and followers who supported me and gave weight to my words by reading them. Without you, the words mean nothing. It's you who make it worth it. Thank you.

And to Om, for giving me hope when I thought there would be none. You are the one who started me on a journey to find and use my voice. And I cannot thank you enough for that.

Made in the USA
Middletown, DE
11 July 2020